Praise for
Fighting for Family

"Chris and Julie carry not only a passion for their own family but a unique ability to help others experience it in their own lives. *Fighting for Family* gives readers a front row seat to the intentional ways they are helping others experience the power of belonging. This message reaches beyond the home and into every area of life."

MARK BURNETT, executive producer of *Survivor*, *The Voice*, *Shark Tank*

ROMA DOWNEY, bestselling author, actress, and producer

"There are few people more dedicated to family than these guys. They practice everything they preach, and we don't say that lightly. Their life is reflected in the pages of this gorgeously engaging yet profound book. The message is clear: no matter what, you belong."

DAVID OYELOWO, actor, producer, writer, director

JESSICA OYELOWO, actress, singer, writer, producer

Cofounders of Yoruba Saxon Productions

"Chris and Julie Bennett have been through it all—and are here to give you hope. As they share their own stories through life's toughest challenges, you'll discover that family can truly be a place of love, forgiveness, and belonging."

CANDACE CAMERON BURE, CEO of Candy Rock entertainment, producer, actress, author, and entrepreneur

"If anyone can teach about fighting for family, it's Chris and Julie. They don't just talk the talk; they walk the walk. . . . 10/10—I highly recommend reading this book to learn from the very best humans in the world."

CAITLIN CROSBY, author, founder and CEO of The Giving Keys

"A remarkable guide that reminds us of the timeless essence of what family truly means. . . . The Bennetts' eloquent and expressive depiction of family mirrors the qualities I've always recognized in them: discernment, love, vulnerability, acceptance, and fun!"

DR. SARAH KIRK, national certified counselor

"While reading these pages, you feel like you're sitting at Chris and Julie's dinner table as they beautifully share about not only the value of family and why it's worth fighting for but also expand the definition of what it means through community. If you're looking for encouragement, this book will remind you that you're worthy of belonging and unconditionally loved."

SARAH DUBBELDAM, founder and chief creative officer of *Darling* Magazine and Clothing
STEVE DUBBELDAM, founder and chief executive officer of Wilderness

"I want to be like Chris and Julie when I grow up. I've never seen more passionate, authentic, and effective lovers of people. . . . *Fighting for Family* will undoubtedly change many more. The world is a better place every time someone picks up this book."

CLARK BECKHAM, singer and *American Idol* runner-up, season 14

"Refreshingly transparent, authentic, hopeful, and hilarious, Chris and Julie have given us a gift in *Fighting for Family*. This book is for real people who live in a messy world and long for deep connection. Whether we are single or married, have children or not, we all long to belong, to be seen, to be known, to be loved, and to be included, because God designed us that way. For this reason, fighting for family is a worthy and essential pursuit."

CHRISTINE CAINE, founder, A21 and Propel Women

"To know Chris and Julie Bennett is to know what *Fighting for Family* is all about—because they live it every day! The powerful faith and love they have cultivated within their own family extends far beyond their own walls, creating an environment in which belonging leads to hope, and hope leads to healing and restoration. You will be so blessed by Chris and Julie's inspiring journey."

KELLI MASTERS, NFL sports agent and founder and president of KMM Sports

"Studies show that isolation, sadness, and loneliness are at record highs. The time has never been more right for a book like *Fighting for Family*. Chris and Julie Bennett are not afraid to share the warts, flaws, bumps, and all that being a family can have. They take us by the hand and allow us in on the journey of joy, connectedness, and fulfillment that only family can provide."

KYM DOUGLAS, author, TV host, comedian

"A brave and transparent book that will encourage you, make you laugh, and show you how to build a life of deep, unshakable community with people—whether you're related by blood or not."

STEVEN BAILEY, professional chef
CHRISTINE BAILEY, author of *The Kindred Life*
and host of *The Kindred Life Podcast*
Cofounders of Kindred Farm

"My family and I have had the pleasure of sitting with the whole Bennett family at the table Julie so beautifully describes. On each occasion we leave full to the brim with the hope their vision and understanding of family imparts. A vision and hope so stunningly offered to all who read this book. A vision and hope letting us know that no matter what it looks like or how it finds you, family and belonging are for all of us."

HEATHER AVIS, *New York Times* bestselling author,
narrative shifter, and founder of The Lucky Few

"I couldn't agree more with what the Bennetts express in *Fighting for Family*—creating family and a foundation of home is the summit of life, the key support system in the ups and downs, and the rhythm that can sustain in every moment life brings. . . . This is a must-read!"

LAUREN KENNEDY, wellness advocate and
author of *Your Beautiful Heart*, *Still LOLO*, and *The Clean Sweep*

"I can affirm these aren't just words you are reading. It's a reality lived out. . . . A work where you will be inspired to keep wrestling and hoping for better relationships and family dynamics no matter where you find yourself on the journey."

JONATHAN PITTS, author, pastor,
and president of For Girls Like You Ministries

"If you've ever wondered whether or not you belong, this book is for you! . . . These pages are an invitation to sit at their dining room table and bear witness to the messy, beautiful home and community they've created. It's an invitation to hear their story and learn from their wisdom so you too can build a life you love and a family that's absolutely worth fighting for."

ALLISON TROWBRIDGE, author
and founder/CEO of Copper Books

"Julie and Chris are relentless in their passion for people. The grace by which they honor the humanness in all of us, while gently sounding a call to greatness, is an honor to watch and a gift to read."

JAE HARDWICK, publicist and producer

"This book champions family in the way I have seen the Bennetts do ever since they first began theirs: with depth, meaning, and intention. You will walk away from this book inspired and equipped on how to family with all you've got from exactly where you are."

DEANGELO RHODES, area director,
Boys & Girls Club Oklahoma City
SARAH RHODES, author, speaker, curriculum
developer, special-needs community advocate

"*Fighting for Family* is a powerful book. I can't think of a more important read for the hour at hand. This book will inspire you to love deeper, go the extra mile, and leave a legacy that matters."

MATTHEW BARNETT, pastor of Los Angeles Dream Center

"*Hopeful*, *authentic*, *honest*, and *vulnerable*: words that Chris and Julie have lived by in the two decades that I have known them, and that emanate so beautifully as they sit across from us in the pages of this book. These two have fought for family so faithfully, and I'm grateful their hard-won wisdom is here to guide me—and all of us—on my own climb in this wild terrain called family."

KIMBERLY BATSON, co-owner,
Fabled Bookshop and Café, Waco, TX

"In a time when loneliness has become its own pandemic, Chris and Julie Bennett extend an invitation to their table and an opportunity to discuss what it means to truly belong to each other. *Fighting for Family* warmly bids the reader to walk and talk with guides who know the lifelong trek best. The reader will find more than stories in the pages ahead. They will discover the steady shoulders and reassuring words from faithful guides who promise that the views from the summit of family are always worth the climb."

BECKY THOMPSON, bestselling author

"A must-read for so many reasons. . . . This is a book that shows you that faith can get you through anything, and that love is the most important thing that we have. The Bennetts prove that."

NEAL MCDONOUGH, actor and producer

"Chris, Julie, and their family are living testaments to Philippians 4:13: 'I can do all things through Christ who strengthens me.' Their humility, openhandedness, and kindness even through every single adversity they've encountered is awe-inspiring. The tools they have cultivated from these experiences will not only benefit families but ultimately help bring healing and restoration to them as well."

MATT SALLE, member of the acapella group Pentatonix

"Chris and Julie believe, truly believe, in the power of family, of belonging, of truth, and they fight for it every day. They fight for it in their own family and for each person who crosses their path. They fight for it because they believe it is worth fighting for. Their story reveals—they're right."

DANNY DEWALT, vice president and chief
of staff, Pepperdine University

"If you desire a sense of deeper belonging and real connection in your relationships but feel afraid and untrusting from past hurt, this book is for you. . . I'm going to reference this book time and time again when I need a reminder to face my fears in order to keep reaching out for true connection."

KRISTEN DALTON WOLFE, author of *The Sparkle Effect*, mental
health and professional life coach, and founder of She Gathers

"A beacon of inspiration desperately needed in our society. . . I'm confident this book will be widely shared, reaching individuals and families who are yearning for its transformative message and also being endorsed and share by the known leaders they mentor and inspire. . . . Its impact will be profound."

SARAH PENDRICK, author, host, and
founder of GirlTalk and Life Audit

"A testament to the resilience of the human spirit and the unbreakable bonds of family . . . The book's blend of humor and poignancy captivates the reader, seamlessly weaving laughter with tears in a beautifully honest narrative. The inclusion of actionable steps at the end of each chapter is a thoughtful touch, providing readers with tangible ways to apply the lessons learned. . . . Above all, the impact this family has made on others is a beautiful tribute to the power of human connection and the enduring strength of love."

MARCYLLE COMBS, writer, speaker, and owner of Mac Legacy

Fighting *for* Family

Fighting *for* Family

The Relentless Pursuit of Building Belonging

JULIE AND CHRIS BENNETT

HARPER HORIZON

ISBN 978-0-7852-9320-0 (ePub)
ISBN 978-0-7852-9319-4 (HC)

Library of Congress Control Number: 2023947029

Printed in the United States of America
23 24 25 26 27 LBC 5 4 3 2 1

This book is dedicated to our four amazing kids: Beau, Nate, Brooks, and Joy. You will always be worth fighting for.

Contents

Introduction, or "Who Are These Guys?"

(Julie)

Hi.

We are so glad you picked up this book, at this time, because we've written it with all our hearts. For you.

"We" are Chris and Julie. What we'd love for you to do is to imagine that you are here with us, at our home. It really is the best place to talk about the serendipitous turns life takes in order to make connection, and how stunning and hard finding one another in the middle of our busy lives, which tend to favor temporary over enduring connection, really is. So imagine we are sitting across from you at our rectangular wooden dining table. Above us hangs a thrift-store chandelier, which you may assume we spent hundreds of dollars on, and we've flipped the dimmer switch on the side wall for ambience. In the corner stands our struggling fiddle-leaf fig (third one this year), which constantly looks as if it's pleading with us to put it out of its misery. Behind us are a plethora of wine bottles available to grab for any occasion, along with a jar full of Sharpie-stained corks on which we've written the reason each bottle of wine was opened and enjoyed: birthdays, new jobs, overcoming hard days, beating cancer—all the things worth celebrating are there because we don't want to forget. Oh, and of course we also have coffee and tea, if that's your jam, because we love those too.

Before me I have a little pile of snack crackers, like Almond Nut-Thins, and a bowl of blueberries, because they are often some of the only foods allowed on my crazy postcancer diet. Chris's meticulously made cup of coffee is growing cold on the table.

Within earshot of the table are our four fantastic kids. Beau the Brilliant is our wise nineteen-year-old tattoo artist and entrepreneur. Nate the Great is our eighteen-year-old resilient leader who just recently committed to play quarterback at our alma mater, Baylor University. (Sic 'em, Bears!) Brooks the Magnificent is our fourteen-year-old enthusiastic entertainer, whom I have always described as Tigger in the body of a boy with a heart of gold. And Joy the Wonder is our honest twelve-year-old daughter who is a blossoming writer and articulate communicator.

We interrupt each other. Our kids interrupt us. Our dog also interrupts us because he's a little goldendoodle puppy that won't quit.

We are at this table because we want to hear your story, hear about what family means to you. Chris and I believe that family is for everyone, and we would love to learn about how family has shown up (or maybe not) for you.

(Chris)

This book is about the beauty and mess of family and why it is worth fighting for. No matter who you are, there's a seat just for you. It's our reflection on the decades we've been building a family together and with others, our memories of how we have overcome the sun-blistered moments life has brought.

We know there is a laundry list of family types: nuclear families, single-parent families, extended families, childless families, stepfamilies, friend families, school families—truly, the list could go on and on because a family can be biological or adopted or chosen and still have the same amount of deep love and connection. That's because family is about choice more than DNA. For many of us, our families of origin have *not* been the primary way we experience unconditional love and belonging.

Maybe you left your home for college with a broken relationship between yourself and a parent, but with time and healing, you want to begin rebuilding it. Or you simply live far away from your family of origin and are attempting to build yourself a new life with friends from work or friends who share in your hobbies. Perhaps you adopted or fostered children and brought them into your home with unreserved affection—in which case, *we* want to read *your* book. You might be at a place where you are part of a vibrant community and you want to go deeper together in health. That's *awesome*; we love that. You might have lost friends and family in the outbreak of division from the last few years, and you wonder whether you can ever trust again. We have watched as the political divisiveness of our nation has gone to new heights—or, rather, new depths—over the last decade. You might have felt alone your whole life and you're trying to figure out how to change that. Whatever your situation, *you are welcome here*. We like you.

Family has as many types and possibilities as one has the ability to imagine. And it can be found wherever you are, with whomever you choose. Julie and I have defined and redefined *family* in every era since we were twenty-one years old, trying to figure it all out. Early on, when we were youth leaders, radio show hosts, counselors, and eventually pastors, *family* meant the people around us, doing those things with us. Then we left all that behind to write and develop new media content in Los Angeles, and suddenly those instant connections that came from being a part of a church community were no longer available. We had to form relationships in Los Angeles that had nothing to do with working in churches, which taught us so much. Now we've been married twenty-three years and have recently landed back in pastoring at a church in Malibu. Truthfully, we are still reworking our definition of *family*, because it seems to be more a feeling than a fact.

We were so full of life and wonder in those early days, ready to conquer the world. And then, before we knew it, the world started to conquer us. We were reminded that family isn't some formula to frantically grab ahold of when the wheels fall off. It's a thousand choices we make again and again, each one transforming us.

We have conquered and overcome a lot, and we have stories to tell here at our table. But that doesn't mean we have arrived; it means we know the terrain. Let's leave our table and go look out the window at what we are about to tackle: the Everest of endeavors.

The Climb

Our lives could be seen as a mountain range. Some mountains we scale, take a picture, and get the heck off them; other mountains we climb for our whole lives. For Julie and me, building a loving, connected home and family is the summit. The goal. Our life's work. And we will never stop climbing this mountain, even if we get drop-kicked down to the foot.

It's not easy. At the base of this range, we think there should be a huge sign like they have at national parks.

UPCOMING

Elevation: 30,000 feet

Full of adventure. Risky.

Difficulty: All—Beginner to Expert

Hikers may experience unknown danger, pain, disappointments, setbacks, disillusionment, and fear, but also great joy, growth, relationships, encouragement, perseverance, and hope.

Julie and I have come face-to-face with this sign so many times—sometimes pondering it painfully while other times reading it with great anticipation. It would be easy for our minds to wander to the expenses that have accrued over the years—to our bodies, our emotional well-being, our bank accounts, our hearts—in our frail attempts, our starts and finishes, to scale this mountain. But we remain committed.

Dehydration, leg cramps, fatigue, disagreements on which way to go and how to do this family trek—these and other challenges have made us want to quit over the years. We have learned that though our failures make us want to blame the mountain over and over again, we are the only ones who can choose to heal and acclimate to begin another painstaking, adventurous climb.

We understand that developing relationships—and staying in them—is hard work, and that work affects us all so differently. Reaching the summit of a mountain can be daunting and treacherous with lots of unknowns, despite all the preparation. Relationships are the same way. You can train, study the terrain, and plan your route, but you still have to get out there and do the work, forcing yourself to push past the pain and discomfort because you are convinced that the journey will be worth it.

(Julie)

Chris is right. Mountain views can be so palpably restful, painfully mundane, but the next moment wonderfully invigorating. On days when I have gone on real mountain hikes, I have woken early, my eyes still half-shut as I begrudgingly tie my boots, wondering if leaving my bed so early was worth it. Yet with every climb, I discover an array of spectacular stone shapes, the carved wear and tear of tree trunks and their broken limbs, the extravagant painting of a day's sunrise, or fragrant flowers growing in rare places. It reminds me why I keep hiking.

This is why I keep fighting for family. The views are magnificent. I have peeked through the door of my daughter's bedroom just to watch the magic of her imagination come alive, and as the sun has gone down, cherished the stillness of her body falling fast asleep. I've opened my door to see my best friend who has driven over six hours to get to me in the middle of my chemotherapy treatment. I've savored staying up extra late just to hear my teenagers process life while being inspired by their honest voices. I've looked through our kitchen window into the backyard, watching while Chris so effortlessly pulls the heartstrings of his children through intentional questions that are laced with sincerity and safety, always propelling them to a deeper understanding of love. What I have seen is beyond compare.

We keep discovering it's worth it. Every. Time. And we truly believe you will too.

If you're a *Harry Potter* fan, you might remember the spectacular scene in the first movie that shows the power of relentless invitation. Harry is an orphan living with his terribly cruel and jealous aunt and uncle, and one day he receives a mailed invitation to attend Hogwarts School of Witchcraft and Wizardry. His uncle immediately confiscates the letter and destroys it with great delight right in front of Harry. The next day another invitation comes and then another, each one maniacally torn up and burned by Harry's uncle. But no matter how hard he tries to keep Harry from those letters, they keep coming. One Sunday, when Uncle Dursley thinks the invitations have finally stopped, the letters begin to flood through the house, flying through the windows and the fireplace—the invitation is unstoppable. Harry gets the message and enters into a future full of promise.[1]

Maybe your self-defense is to behave like Harry's aunt and uncle, trying desperately to burn every invitation to experience something more in family. Maybe you're afraid of change. Yet the invitations keep coming. We hope as you read each chapter of this book that, regardless of your situation, you'll let your defenses down and accept that you are wanted, needed, and invited into a future full of connection.

Family is really hard. It will cost you your time, your money, your comfort, your security, and sometimes, even your ideals. But I promise you that there will always be a reward at the end of the climb. At the very least, you will grow and change. Through the hard times and misunderstandings your endurance and your capacity to serve others will grow, and so will your appreciation for how far you have come. This will push you to keep going.

But there will be setbacks. Part of our family's climb has involved battling breast cancer. I've beaten it twice; first in 2018 and then in 2020. I remember my first hike shortly after completing chemotherapy treatments for my second bout with cancer. I was excited to conquer the day, hopeful I was finished with the hardest stretch of cancer I had experienced so far. I walked with a strut to the starting point because I was so confident in how great I happened to be feeling that day. I felt a rush of satisfaction heading up the first incline, almost reaching the first turn. Los Angeles isn't known for its rain, but we had experienced a rare and generous outpouring the previous months, which had caused a plethora of greens that were exploding around me. I was enjoying detailed blooms as I moved in a fast rhythm, proud of my stamina.

And then it hit me. My glorious strength left me after five minutes of being on the trail. Everything hurt; my muscles that were just moving so freely felt like they had gotten stuck in molten lava. It was as if chemo was taunting me, sneering as I kept trying to move forward. I felt a whirlwind of anger and sadness and grief swirling through my mind and body. I was stunned, then down for the count. I had to turn around, and I was mad about it. I wanted to finish. I wanted to accomplish what I had come there for. But I had to go down, back to base camp, to rest, heal, and regroup to be able to head back up again.

Sometimes going backward is necessary in order to go forward. I've learned never to resent the beauty of base camp. My visits there help me to keep growing, like a good stretch gets me loose before a climb.

Wherever you're starting in your journey toward family, that's your base camp. Don't knock it. Don't discount where you've come from. Take time to stretch, to dream of what you'll find as you search for your family, the one you make for yourself. There is more of the mountain to climb, peaks yet to be reached, views that will remind you there is more—more to your relationships, more to your community.

As we walk through these chapters, we will explore the ankle-breaking and awe-inspiring themes of adventure; allowing imperfection; setting a table of honor; embracing mess; and building humility and boundaries, forgiveness and service. Our hope is that you make space to rest, reflect, and refuel at each point before moving on to the next chapter.

Maybe it's time to pull out your old journal and remember how far you have come in some friendships, go to coffee with a person you need to reconnect with and reflect on the good times you had, invite a neighbor over for dinner, or sit down with someone who is very different from you simply to listen and learn. Small steps are your new best friend. Don't be in a hurry—every day is a new opportunity to learn and start over. Give yourself and those around you time. We want you to come away from this book with the belief that you can and will build (and maintain) more connections, which will keep you humble, joyful, and full of purpose.

Do you remember playing hide-and-seek? "Home base" was the only place where you couldn't be called out. You would wait for the seeker to be distracted, then crawl, run, and leap over a coffee table or any obstacle in the way to get there. We are all looking for home base. Chris and I are writing this book because at times we have failed to create a home base, or safe place, for people and have been unable to find our own. But we know that it's possible—not just possible but necessary. You must have a place you can be fully yourself.

We are writing this book for the people who are still looking for those home bases, who have given up that such a place even exists. We are writing this book because we have tasted family, and it's addictive. Chris and I have failed at being family at times but know it's worth getting back up and trying again and again. We are writing this book because we think it matters just about as much as anything else in the world. And mostly, we are writing this book because we believe that everyone deserves to belong.

The *New York Times* recently published an article by John Leland titled "How Loneliness Is Damaging Our Health," which stated that "even before the pandemic, there was an 'epidemic of loneliness,' and it was affecting physical health and life expectancy."[2] And this epidemic seems to be spreading faster and farther than ever before. Loneliness is a chronic illness that needs the cure of family.

You are not alone. There are all sorts of people like us trying to keep up our courage to build a family. In our differences, preferences, and alikeness, we will find each other. We call each other up this mountain. No one can ever make or coerce you to fight for family if you don't want to. But your pain and disappointments don't have to have the final word. This beautiful and wild life of loving others opens its palms and invites you in. Come with us. Let's learn the ways we can belong, together.

Chapter 1

The Great Adventure

*To refuse the adventure is to run the risk
of drying up like a pea in its shell.*
—GEORGE LEIGH MALLORY

(Julie)

Here We Go

Every great adventure begins with a feeling of unease—that woozy, sick feeling you get before jumping off a cliff into the sparkling lake below. The water is crisp and blue, and your hot, tired skin knows that the moment of impact will be worth every millisecond spent falling through the air. And yet the body often says no. What has always helped me has been having a friend up there on the ridge with me to say those fateful five words: "I'll jump if you jump."

I can take a risk much more easily if I'm with someone else, and for over twenty years, that someone else has been Chris. Pretty quickly (we married young), it came to include Beau, Nate, Brooks, and Joy. Let me tell you about a risk we chose (the move to Los Angeles) and one we didn't (cancer). They happened at almost the same time.

I can still remember the moment in the blazing-hot summer of 2018 when we pulled out of our Norman, Oklahoma, driveway and made the final loop around the cul-de-sac where we had lived for the previous seven years. In the rearview mirror was our battle-worn basketball goal cemented in between our yard and our neighbors' (our best friends) yard. There's no video evidence, but Chris swears that over the years there were a couple of epic shots that would have impressed Steph Curry. The fiberglass backboard was partially shattered from years of neighborly competitions of "Let's see who can launch the basketball from across the street and make it." To save money and time, Chris had hoisted one of the boys up on his shoulders and used a roll of Beau's endless supply of duct tape to secure a piece of cardboard over the missing glass. I could also see the tree swing we had put up years earlier, where we had spent countless hours pushing Joy and her friends in dizzying circles. All those memories—we were leaving them behind.

We had spent nearly a decade as pastors, building a growing church with a big staff. Norman is not a big town, but it's not a small one either. It's the kind of place where you will bump into your neighbors at the grocery store and will have no trouble carpooling with friends to get the kids to school. It will take a few

4

weeks to burn through a tank of gas because all that you need exists in that medium-size town.

Our church was filled with people of all different age groups, ethnicities, and economic backgrounds—and, of course, a horde of college kids. Norman is home to the University of Oklahoma, with a student population of thirty thousand. On Saturdays in the fall, when there is a home football game, the town turns into a cathedral with more than ninety thousand worshippers cheering for the Sooners. As for our church, it was the kind of place people looked forward to showing up to on a Sunday morning. Chris made sure that our café had the right vibe and the best coffee beans in town.

For years we had pitched a vision to our community that we were not just an organization or a bunch of people in a building, but a family. Yet we constantly lived with a sense that we were under-delivering on our idealistic dream, even with the best of intentions. We were tired from the previous years of managing people and carrying loads of responsibility, and we were genuinely excited to enter into a new season in a new city. There was more for each of us, we felt, than the "easy like Sunday morning" life that we had, and each member of our family had a desire to try to "make it" somewhere else. We wanted to test limits, and we knew if we stayed in Norman, that wasn't going to happen.

The kids, who were fourteen, twelve, nine, and seven at the time, were genuinely excited. We were intentional about making sure our kids had the same peace regarding the move as we did. And "peace" didn't mean that the nerves were not there—they were. But this is how we like to make our big choices: together as a family. And while we are aware that each of our kids carries a certain level of maturity and understanding, we deeply value their individual voices, perspectives, and especially their feelings. This wasn't going to impact only Chris and me but would profoundly impact them all. Their best friends had been our neighbors, classmates, and fellow church members.

We knew even back then that moving is one of the three biggest stressors (deaths, divorces, and moves) a person (much less a family) can go through,[1] so you would think that we had a pretty strong reason to do it, but we didn't. There was no job offer or firing that had led to this decision. Instead, our weary and hopeful hearts had latched on to little hints that what we wanted was hiding on the West Coast, land of music and film and creative groups galore. We wanted to build community with others, not as pastors but as a family ready to explore the power of belonging through media and entertainment in one of the largest, most disconnected cities in the world: Los Angeles.

We had packed up everything to be put in storage at our destination, and we'd piled into our cars. Chris and I were leaving the place where we had raised our kids and the church we had built. We were driving away from friends, neighbors, and family. And the only thing stronger than our sadness was our overwhelming excitement for a new start and a new adventure. We had stars in our eyes.

We spent two days making the drive to where we planned to temporarily lodge at the home of a family whom Chris had briefly met through some friends. Jim and Suzy Frankian are the kind of people you want to live on the same street with. Their home is nestled on a picturesque street with large, overhanging trees, giving the pavement unending shade. There is literally a white picket fence wrapped around the front yard. We rolled up in our fleet of vehicles with our mounds of unmatched baggage and made our way to the front door. By the next evening, Suzy was staying up extra late to help decorate for Chris's fortieth birthday. That's a big birthday to celebrate only two nights into a new city. Beau and Nate were starting their new school, and I was going to try my hand at homeschooling Brooks and Joy. We were wide-eyed and excited, wondering where we would end up living after the fortnight we had planned there with the Frankians.

And so our new life began. We had chosen to be an adventurous family. Then life gave us no choice in being a brave one.

Unraveling Plans

Our intended two-week stay turned into nine weeks. The contract on our home in Oklahoma fell through, so the money we were going to use from the sale was not going to be available anytime soon. We had notified our gracious hosts that we were going to be moving out on November 9, regardless of our circumstances, so we didn't overstay our welcome. And then, little more than a week before we were set to leave Jim and Suzy's house, I went to the doctor to check up on a troubling lump underneath my right armpit. The day before we were to move out, I got a call while driving home. I had stage 3 metastatic breast cancer.

I was stunned, as though a paintball gun had just shot me from behind. I felt dazed and heartbroken, but those words barely describe the intensity of my initial emotions. I remember one of the first thoughts I had: *Pull it together, Julie,* I snarled at myself, over and over, as the waves of grief hit me in the car.

I called Chris with the news. Even though we were talking about it while I drove, we were both in complete shock. *This is not what we had dreamed at all. What about our future? What about our kids? Cancer*—this one word had upended our lives, and we thought we had already done that by moving. Now we weren't just in transition. We were in crisis.

I pulled up in front of the Frankians' house and stared blankly at the picturesque white picket fence as Chris made his way to the car. He leaned over and gave me a hug of security and comfort while we both just cried and hugged for what seemed like an hour. He got in the passenger side; we needed time alone to process the news before facing the kids. As we sat in the car together, Chris posed the obvious question: "Should we go back to Oklahoma and regroup?"

It was a legitimate question. Our friends and family would ask the same thing. Right away I could imagine them saying, "Stop being crazy and come back now!" I needed to start chemotherapy within the next two weeks; neither of us had jobs, and we had nowhere to live. But Chris's question started a rumbling fire inside me, and I'm pretty sure I cut him off midsentence.

"We have been led here, to LA. God knows us. God knew I had cancer before we moved, but I think we found out here because otherwise we would never have come. We aren't going anywhere. We will go through this together."

He looked at me and saw resolve in my eyes. Our great risk just got riskier, but in that moment, we doubled down. We would stay. We would walk through this—all six of us—together. I didn't have to do this alone.

If that sounds like insanity to you, take a number and get in line. A handful of people thought we had lost our minds, and they let us know they believed we had "missed God" (or to others, "ignored the universe") and were being selfish to put our kids through this crucible. But they didn't understand that we knew these choices would be the making of us. We wanted to thrive under pressure in Los Angeles. We didn't want to coast in Oklahoma any longer, not ever knowing who each of us could truly be if we just tried something new. Our choice may sound irresponsible, but we were that confident in our dreams and our purposes. We wanted to stay in the story.

(Chris)

Family Doesn't Play It Safe

You may be reading this and thinking, *Julie is crazy. Who in the world would want to stay in LA without a home and any real security while dealing with cancer?* Well, you don't know my wife (yet). I have seen her determined face on countless occasions. She's not fearless; she just chooses hope over fear. I was fully prepared to head back to Oklahoma if that was what she wanted, but it wasn't, and I didn't want it either. So we did what we always do: we made a decision and then didn't look back. Fundamental to this capacity of taking risks in the midst of adversity is the strength of our relationship. We *can* risk because we have each other.

Julie and I don't want to play life safe, but it's not an easy task, especially when you have a whole family involved. When we were kids, most of us didn't think twice about taking a risk; it took only a couple of stumbles and tumbles, though, before we started to hold back. Is there wisdom in this? Sure. But sometimes fear can mask itself as wisdom. The older we get, the safer we want to be. We look for stability and comfort, we live for a paycheck, we settle, and if we aren't careful, we end up in a *Groundhog Day* life with no clue how to get out of it. Too many of us have moved on from "What if?" to "Oh well." But "What if?" sends us out to possibilities. It's a way of life.

When I was in high school in Texas, I had a group of friends I called my "band of brothers." For senior graduation we begged our parents to let us go on the trip of a lifetime, or what felt that way at the time. We somehow got Steven Bailey's mom to loan us her forest green 1994 Ford Aerostar van to make the cross-country trek from Dallas to Destin, Florida, and back again.

Just before we had loaded up our luggage and filled up the tank with gas that was $1.23 per gallon (true and heartbreaking story), I made the boldest and most rebellious decision of my life. I got an earring. Not sure what I was thinking, as I've always been a little self-conscious about my ears ever since being called "Dumbo" in sixth grade. My little silver hoop only brought my ears extra unwanted attention. The earring lasted only a few months, but I still have an eternal hole punch to remind me of my choice. And my kids won't let me forget it either.

Crammed into this middle-aged people mover with the back row intentionally removed to create somewhat of a lounge area termed "the cage," we left town. With no GPS or smartphones and my sense of no direction, it is a miracle that we ever made it.

We stopped in Tuscaloosa, Alabama, to connect with some friends we had met at a camp the summer before. (Yes, I may have written a lengthy letter to one of them expressing my love and intention to marry her one day. It wasn't fully reciprocated. Must have been the earring.) We ate fall-off-the-ribs barbecue in North Carolina and spent a night with one of my friends' grandmothers. We drove through the Blue Ridge Mountains with the windows rolled down. Blaring through the buzzing speakers from a cassette tape was James Taylor, singing "Carolina in My Mind." We were belting out the words like oblivious contestants on *American Idol*. We stopped on the side of the road and stared out into the Smoky Mountains as the clouds were gently dangling over the top of the ridge, and we didn't say a word. A holy moment.

Once we made it to the bleach-white shores of Destin, the boys and I played hours of paddleball on the beach, applied zero sunscreen, and kept reminding one another to "bounce the eyes" among all the bikini-clad ladies.

Every time I tell this story, I can feel the sense of wanderlust coming back. I never wanted the trip to end. The banter, slapping our faces to keep from falling asleep at the wheel, and trying not to pee our pants laughing at inappropriate adolescent jokes—all these shared life experiences were not only memorable but forged a strength in our friendships that remains today. It changed us forever. Those are feelings I want everyone to experience and hold on to, and our choices can bring us closer to or further from them.

We need markers of "back when" to remember how worth it the work, the strangeness, the sense of "what's going to happen now" all are. Takings risks and seeking adventures with others have a way of forming bonds that stand the test of time. And if you're wondering whether you take risks because you have family or if family is forged because of the risks you take—the answer is both.

Julie and I will sit on the couch with feet up and laugh as we remember the spontaneity of our early years together: leaving at midnight to find the twenty-four-hour IHOP in the next town over, eating all the bacon and pancakes we could stomach, and then crashing at four in the morning to sleep the day away. Walmart stops midday to buy our new favorite CD and then driving aimlessly until we finished every song on the album.

Now we are deep into marriage and kids, so you would think that we transformed into people with meticulous schedules and jam-packed planners, but as many activities as we do have, we still love to refrain from planning if we can help it.

If our lives were a coloring book, we Bennetts would be coloring way outside the lines. The "lines" are the responsible questions, such as these:

- Will other people understand our decision?
- Is it safe?
- Can we really afford it?
- Can we be sure it will work out?

These questions show up late (if at all) in the Bennett decision-making paradigm, and you can tell the outcome by looking at our lives. Sometimes it works out like a sparkly Kandinsky painting (like getting to write this book!), and sometimes it ends up like a kid's drawing on the fridge. But we love all the art we've made, and we wouldn't have it any other way.

Although we rearrange our priorities so "safety" isn't number one, it doesn't mean everyone should live like us. But it sure has shaped us. Our story wouldn't be the same if we were "safety first." We will keep asking questions, staying curious, healing, and laughing, but we will also keep taking risks and looking for new adventures, big and small.

(Julie)

When It All Goes Up in Smoke

A friend recently shared with us that the mind is most motivated not by the prospect of what could happen if you take a risk but by what could happen if you *didn't*. So once you have played out the countless unpredictable scenarios in your brain, settled your breath, and processed with those you trust, there is nothing left for you to do but take the leap. This takes courage, no matter your personality type.

Chris is an idealist and a cup-half-full person, and I am similar. We have spent many days dreaming and setting our minds to believe for big things, only to realize that life rarely plays out like the Oscar-worthy, feel-good script we have written in our minds.

When we left our world in Oklahoma to move to California, we had no idea what was ahead of us, but in our minds it was a chapter of our story titled "Boundless Opportunities." The chapter would be all about receiving a kind of bountiful harvest from the hard years we had already been through. We envisioned open doors to things we had newly and long been dreaming of—a sort of serene rest and a smooth reset of life. That wasn't what happened.

A few months and four or five rentals after the diagnosis, we were still trying to find a permanent home. The housing situation in Los Angeles is *insane*, between the cost of living, finding a home, and actually moving in. I was a few rounds into chemotherapy by this time, my hair was beginning to come out in large clumps, and the family morale was low. We arrived at that week's rental and began to do what we always did: unload our carefully packed Suburban onto the driveway. Once we got inside, ready to sit down and take a deep breath, we were overcome with the pungent smell of cigarette smoke. It reeked on every surface; it was inescapable. I was pissed. There was no way I could stay there with my nausea. We would have to go.

We were tired and frustrated and at the end of our ropes. As Chris begrudgingly began to reload our bags in his *Tetris*-like way into the Suburban, I felt the weight of the situation. But something else hit me. I could see Brooks trapped in between a mound of baggage, looking like a coal miner whose cave had crashed in. I glanced at my bedraggled appearance in the car window. I began to hysterically laugh. I mean, out-of-control laugh. Was I losing my mind and my hair at the same time? As Chris looked at me with my patchy scalp and crazy eyes, peeing myself with uncontrollable laughter, he couldn't help but join me. It all felt so absurd. The giggles became contagious. Soon, every member of the family was in on it, laughing and slapping the air. We were, as they say, giddy with exhaustion. The medicine of laughter had arrived. We had no clue where we would lay our heads down that night. But we were laughing. We had nothing, not even a home, but we had each other. It was a bit of a revelation, really.

The feelings we get when we live courageously are what not only make life worth living but are a necessary nourishment to keep us healthy and thriving. We need the incomparable rush of what road trips and big changes can bring us. As a pastor, Chris would often tell our previous church, "If you feel like God is nudging you to do something, say yes before you know *how.*" For us, our faith is linked to great, wild choices. But even if this isn't the framework you operate in, there's something to be said for jumping in—and staying the course—even when you don't have everything figured out. And nothing beats the decision to build relationships. Our discovery has been that family doesn't just go *on* the adventure; they *are* the adventure. Nothing else can give you the highs and lows of intimate friendships, of the choice to stay when you could go, to forgive when you could hold on to bitterness. As the proverb says, "If you want to go fast, go alone. If you want to go far, go together."

Find Your Katy

Remember that montage in *Dumb and Dumber* when Harry and Lloyd are making their cross-country trek to "a place where the beer flows like wine, where beautiful women instinctively flock like the salmon of Capistrano"?[2] They ditch the legendary, gas-guzzling Mutt Cutts van for the more intimate and economical motorbike that could get seventy miles per gallon. Lloyd wears Harry like a bulky backpack as they pass through endless wheat fields and then into the frigid Colorado mountains. While on the motorbike, Harry urinates (Lloyd appreciates the warmth), and Lloyd's snot freezes to his upper lip. I have loved that incredibly juvenile, slapstick movie since eighth grade. The two men chose to take their ridiculous, ill-planned adventure *together*—snot, pee, and all. And that's a good picture for how Chris and I do family, to be honest. We're both determined to have this "in it until the end" mentality with our people, and it has kept us together and (partially) sane. We know that this is the only way to write our story.

We make choices about who gets to go to the snot stations with us. We need to have at least one of those people close by at all times. These are the people who show up when we are at your weakest, lowest, and most vulnerable. Chris and I realize that for many of you, no one showed up when you needed them the most. Those who you thought would be there were nowhere to be found. Our point remains—we *need* people to show up when we want to give up. And while there is no formula for meeting this need, our hope is that this book can give you some tools to cultivate these types of relationships and connections. Even deeper than that, as we try to find the people we want to go through our biggest highs and lows with, there are values and character traits that we can work on, in ourselves, to give our relationships their greatest chance. We've learned about some of them from the people in our lives—like my friend Katy.

Since we were young, Katy has taught me how to love others past my pain, in my pain, when I have really blown it, and when I'm feeling betrayed, rejected, judged, and unseen. She has weathered the storms with me since our freshman year of high school, when I met her in gym class. She walked into the locker room with those striking blue eyes, pinched rolled jeans, long California-blonde hair, the most genuine smile you've ever seen, and a presence that says you're always welcome. With no exaggeration, I can say that from that day forward, she became "home" for me. And not just for me but eventually for our whole family. She is Aunt Katy, who has shown up for all of us—depleting her savings to get me counseling when I felt frozen and was barely staying afloat, offering financial help at our most vulnerable times, taking my daughter to dinner when she needed another female voice. Anytime I am in crisis, my Kate is always the first place I go. She's also the one who is my green light to adventures like last-minute road trips across the US with barely enough money for gas, or overcoming fears by bungee jumping with forged parents' signatures. She has never batted an eye on my worst days—when she heard the worst rumors in high school or watched me in destructive patterns. She spoke about me being a hero to her even in the times I wasn't capable of being a good friend. She has loved me in ways that are unfathomable.

I will repeat this until the cows come home: the kind of adventurous life you long for will only be worth it with people like Katy by your side. You must fight to find and keep them. I recognize that Katy, in particular, is a rare gift. But we need people to show up for us, and we have to be open to who may be the answer.

Sometimes it requires us sharing our needs with those around us and inviting others to step in. For example, it was a struggle for me to let people help during my cancer journey because I was so used to being strong and doing things on my own. Cancer forced me to let others in. I learned to let people know what I needed, and it gave them the opportunity to show up. That made me feel vulnerable, but it was necessary.

Maybe you don't have a Katy in your life right now, but I would guess that there is someone who would be willing and able to come alongside you if they were given the chance. Maybe this could be the first risk you take. Or maybe you are like me in another way: seeking to build deeper character in my life to be like Katy. To be dependable, kind, and faithful. It doesn't take much. It can be something as simple as offering a timely hug, sending an encouraging text to a friend you haven't talked to in a while, or lending an ear to a neighbor or someone in need. Sometimes just stopping and listening goes a long way.

Life is much more fun and less terrifying when we take our risks together. Sadly, fear is oftentimes what holds us back, but that's why we need each other. We need other people to look us in the eyes, grab us by the shoulders, and tell us that sure, we aren't perfect, but we are darn well worth love. We need people by our sides, physically and emotionally, to track the days and nights of our journeys on earth. We can witness so many things together: the times when this big climb feels a hundred years long (like waiting at the DMV) and when it flies by and we are dizzy with exhaustion and joy. We need Harry-and-Lloyd-like friends—Katys and name-your-person-here.

(Chris)

All for One and One for All

A couple of years ago, Julie and I invited over a few of our single adult friends to get their perspectives on family. The motivation for this conversation was to hear how they experience family without being married and having children. We acknowledge that, unintentionally, those who are married with children can be elevated in our society to a place of borderline worship. "You've arrived! You made it!" we tell them in our actions and our words. A ring and a baby appear to be the signs of true fulfillment and significance.

Our friend Peta, who had gone through a divorce in her twenties and is very recently remarried to an amazing man, was single at the time we first discussed this with her. We were eating a meal and chatting about the importance of "belonging" within family. She said something that stopped us in our tracks and caused us to rewind so she could say it again. She looked off to the side, back at us again, and said in her characteristically forceful yet soft tone: "Belonging is not something you find; it's something you bring." Whoa. That's a big thought.

The premise of this book is that family is for everyone—not just those married with children but also those who have been lucky enough to find family in one or more of its multifaceted forms. We can't help but find ourselves wondering what our readers who aren't married and don't have kids might be thinking as they make their way through these pages. This curiosity led us to reach out to one of our closest friends, Joshua, who is single.

We go way back—back to the days of Baylor University. My kids call him Uncle Joshua, as they should. He has shown up for birthdays and spontaneous trips. He even took my son on one of his college football recruiting trips. As a single man in his forties, he's one of the most relationally connected and family-oriented people we know, and we have gleaned so much from his life. Recently we asked him how he has built his relationships as a single person.

He was brutally honest, as always, about the challenges of being unattached. He has a respectable job and lives in a beautiful home in a desirable neighborhood. We have been on the receiving end of being a guest in his home on multiple occasions. He loves to have people over for dinner and sit around the table talking until the wee hours over a bottle of wine and a brilliant meal he has made. But at the end of the night, he goes to bed and wakes up to an empty house and, at times, an empty feeling on the inside.

Joshua shared a question he'd recently asked himself and acknowledged that it sounded a bit morbid: "If I died at home or had a bad accident, how long would it take for someone to notice? For someone to find me?" This hit me hard. I've never had that thought in my entire life, likely because I am constantly, and I mean *constantly*, surrounded by Bennetts. I can't get five minutes alone in my house. He continued: "In our society, marriage and family are the entry points to so many opportunities to connect. Kids are a gateway to a whole world of relationships and activities that no one thinks to invite singles to. And once your friends get married, there are so many dinners and events that couples get invited to and singles just don't. No one explains why it's only couples, and no one really knows. It just is." Wow. As someone who got married at twenty-one, I never considered this, which validates his point. He wasn't bitter and jealous; he was just telling the truth.

He went on to talk about his choice not to dwell on the things he lacks but to focus on gratefulness and appreciation for what he has in his friends. He gave an example: When he sees pictures of families on social media around the holidays, it can bring up a sense of loneliness and lack. He talked about how he cannot and should not ignore those feelings, because they are real. But he is also really grateful for these friends and their kids, so he will vocalize that—literally say it out loud in the room, or call and tell them, or comment on the picture about how he loves them. He is authentically living in the tension of lack and love that keeps him vulnerable. It is that vulnerability he holds that helps him model family like few people I have ever met. We asked him his secret to how he cultivates his life:

"Intentionality."

He said it forcefully. Joshua has chosen to make certain proactive decisions with intentionality instead of waiting for others to take the lead. Rather than moving somewhere for a job, he moved for relationships. He chose to buy a house in a particular neighborhood because it is filled with families who are out and about in the evenings with their kids and because he already had several friends who lived within a few minutes' walk. When he is feeling lonely and stuck, he often chooses to go on a walk, knowing he will bump into a familiar face, which often leads to a spontaneous invite for dinner or to a kid's soccer game. He also will drop by a friend's house just to say hey, or hop on a plane for a last-minute trip to visit friends. He uses his evening commute or time doing yard work or cooking to call friends for no other reason than to catch up. Joshua has chosen a life of intention because he desires a sense of family that deeply. While he may not be Bennett flesh and blood, he is family to us.

Just this past week I had a long-overdue coffee meeting with a member of the local church that I pastor. What I learned was a hard pill to swallow. The church talks a lot about being a family and a place of belonging. We believe it and do our best to create a hospitable and welcoming environment for everyone, which is why it was so painful to hear what I did. This precious woman, Carrie, is single, in her forties, and has been attending our community for more than a year. Carrie shared with me the pain of standing around after our services, waiting to see if anyone would notice her, speak to her, show her that she belongs. And while dozens of people laughed and connected all around her, she stood there week after week feeling alone and invisible. She said she began to believe a lie: she didn't belong. Carrie went on to share how she went home after church one day and prayed about what she should do. What she said next stunned me: "I felt that I was to go find the people who were alone and felt like me and show them that they belong." And that's what she has been doing—finding the lonely and isolated and intentionally working to build meaningful connection. She could have been bitter and angry at the church, at me, at the world, but she chose to be courageous and bring belonging to others. I was in tears. What if we all had this kind of mindset and willingness in our pursuit to create a place of family?

So what do Peta's mic-drop comment about belonging and Joshua's radical intentionality and Carrie's bold decision have to do with adventure and risk? Just a couple of years ago Peta took the biggest risk of her life by stepping into a new relationship with an amazing man who was recently widowed with four girls. They are now married, and she continues to bravely navigate these unchartered relational waters. Joshua has literally traveled the world—from backpacking across Patagonia to touring "the Shire" from *Lord of the Rings* in New Zealand—but never alone. He has invited and often funded a friend or family member to join him on his Magellan-like explorations. And Carrie stepped beyond her insecurities and reached out to pull others in. We have watched as all three have refused to let others limit their desire for adventure and have repeatedly jumped off the cliff of uncertainty, all with great intention.

Invitation to Intentionality

Would you join us as we take some timid yet courageous steps toward believing in family again, or maybe for the first time? We know you have a unique story that is your own. We are writing this book with the confident hunch that you are looking to strengthen the family you have or find the one you have never had. We realize you may not have a family like ours, one that has battled through sickness and moving. You may not have had a Katy in your life or a band of brothers to traverse across the country with. But here's what we all have in common: *we were made for family*, and we are better off when we find it.

So as we grab our backpacks, put on our hiking shoes, and brace ourselves for the daunting mountains of family, we are going together. Our hope is that this book will help you to discover some clues on the map that will lead you to the treasure that is family. So would you do us and yourself a favor? Come with an open heart and an open mind. Lay down your negative preconceptions of what family is or what it never could be. Stay with us and re-imagine what your life could look like, and especially feel like, in a place of unconditional love and belonging. That's where we are headed, but it's going to take a lot of risk, fortitude, and humility to get there. We can promise you that it will be worth it.

In his book *You're Invited*, Jon Levy provides some great insight in how to begin building belonging with others. Jon points out that one of the best ways to start with someone new is to propose an activity together, like inviting a neighbor over to cook a meal with you or offering to join a coworker for their pickleball game.[3] When you find common ground with another person, regardless of your differences, a sense of meaningful connection can form. Over time, a shared activity can grow into friendship and even become a budding community as others are invited in. So what is something you love to do that is easy and life-giving? Who could you invite to join you in this experience? If you've given it a try and it didn't work, consider taking the risk again. Try a new person or a new activity. We think you will be pleasantly surprised with what you find.

Getting Started

Take out a pen and paper and give yourself thirty minutes. Sit and reflect, and then write as freely as you can answers to the following questions:

1. What do you feel when you hear the word *family*?
2. What is a memory you have of a moment when you truly felt like you belonged in a community or group or relationship? How did you feel, and what was present in that relationship?
3. Identify three people in your life whom you have looked in the eye (or wanted to), whom you could take one step to connect with. This could be your local barista, the couple next door, or someone in a class you are taking. Be intentional as you plan the first step, and then do it.

Chapter 2

WTF? (What the Family?)

Nothing in life is fun for the whole family.
—JERRY SEINFELD

(Julie)

Trigger Warnings and Family Language

In the summer of 2019, at the tail end of my first cancer battle, Chris and I held a birthday party for our daughter, Joy, at our friend's home, which was gorgeously decked out with my best version of a Pinterest party acquired at Walmart and the local Dollar Tree. We had mermaid-themed everything (including the napkins), tails made of papier-mâché, and the pool our friend had graciously let us use. That's how we roll. We ain't that fancy.

As we do for every birthday, we invited those gathered to share memories and encouragements for the honored birthday girl. Each person shared a memory or a piece of thoughtful encouragement, and Joy was glowing.

Then it happened. Our new friend Casey, whom we were just getting to know, said some lovely things to Joy and then turned to Chris and me and wrapped up her speech with these words: "And thank you to the Bennetts for making me a part of your family!"

My insides froze a teeny bit.

Wait. Hold up. Who said I made you a part of our family? You are new.

My heart started beating quickly. I felt a bit wobbly. Chris squeezed my hand. As sweet as Casey's intentions were, those words carried an expectation I couldn't handle right then. She wasn't wrong, and what she said was sincere. But I was trying to heal, so I knew we couldn't be "family" for Casey in the ways she needed it. We had no extra space for weekly dinners and late-night talks. It made me want to pull away and run. I had just begun to grapple with the fact that my kids were adjusting to major life changes. And I was working through both the pain caused by people who claimed to be like family but bailed on me when I needed them most, and the shame I carried around from others who said I let them down.

I didn't have any more room for a new "family" member to join our already crowded, maxed-out, bone-dry life. All I could think of were the inevitable ways that we would let her down. My walls were up. I couldn't handle any more pressure, and the language we use to talk about family brings pressure.

We can't deny it. The f-word has become the costliest and most overused word in relationships. We can toss it around for quick intimacy, or we can use it to exact what we want. And each of us brings our past with it. Maybe your idea of family is people who say they love you but don't show up. Maybe it's the opposite, and you think every hangout needs a gift and a card. Who knows? The word is chock-full of meaning.

Chris and I haven't always been good at knowing when to use the word and when not to. To be honest, the Bennett superpower is making strangers *feel* like family. We are intentional with people in our home, but our superpower can be another person's kryptonite. We have limited capacity, and because our words sometimes haven't matched our actions, some people have felt we extended an invitation that we couldn't deliver on. I hear it all the time—people overpromising with language. Like when someone calls you their "bestie" casually and then ignores your texts for a hang. We must be cautious with our language so as not to sign a check that our limits and constraints can't cash.

When I was in college, having a talk with a love interest about the state of the relationship was called "having a D.T.R." (define the relationship). I can't tell you how many of those I have been in over the years—it's embarrassing, to say the least. But I especially remember the conversation that Chris and I had at the modest boat marina at Baylor University, our Sonic vanilla Cokes in hand, where I was fully prepared to break up with him after a short couple of months. Little did I know he came prepared to do the same thing that night. Thankfully, the separation didn't last for long. (Can you fall in love with someone because they are a great hugger? Well, I did.) The moral of the story is that family language is important and necessary but oftentimes clunky.

Yet, even though it often has helped, relationship and family language—whether from my church family, my immediate family, or my friends-circle family—can trigger me. But this journey isn't about never being triggered or demolishing our bad feelings. It's about asking the questions. So Chris and I invite you to take on the motto of the gym around the corner of our house: "Welcome, this is a judgment free zone."[1] So with that pep talk in mind, here's a question we have often asked, whether it sprouts after a deep talk, a late-night movie hang, or in the middle of a shockingly quiet week where we wonder if our friends remember we are even alive: *What does it mean to be "family" anyway?*

(Chris)

Great Expectations

I'd be willing to bet that at some point, you've been so lost, confused, or just irritated at the lack of clarity around this topic that you were like, "What. The. Family?!" What *is* this? What is it meant to be? The f-word provokes a lot of big feelings. To some people, *family* sounds like a cuss word. The word can be a platitude. A trigger word. A wrecking ball. A sweet concession.

When someone comments that you are now "family," how do you feel?

I immediately sense caution in my body—concern that it won't be long before I disappoint that person. It feels like there is a big, fat, heavy coat of expectation being placed on me that I didn't ask to wear. Julie says, as she did in her story about Joy's birthday party, that she gets a twinge of fear. I'm just recently unraveling the sting of the loss of people who were once family and now aren't. In one instance, the pain was from the slow, unspoken realization that a once-tight friendship was no longer what it used to be. Misunderstanding crept in, and the relationship seemed to end quickly without any explanation or a willingness to resolve. My friend was hurt by me, and I didn't know why. *Family*—even though Julie and I both love it enough to write a book about it— is a loaded topic.

Expectations—we all have them. And each of us bring our version of them to relationships. I know you've encountered these obstacles: You gave someone your valuable time, but they only value tangible gifts. You feel inclusion looks like invitations to every event, but your friends are introverts and like to limit their obligations and hang out in small groups. You think being truly close means your people back all your choices, and your people think it means sparring with you over them.

Julie and I understand giving up. Trying to belong is exhausting. You shouldn't have to *try* to belong! But for those who have attempted to, again and again, and come up with the same outcome, giving up on the idea of belonging seems reasonable.

But in this era of isolation, we need to have our expectation glasses cleaned off a bit; we may even need a new prescription! Our talk around family has caused lots of smudges and fogging.

Julie and I have found that unmet expectations around the

meaning of "family" to be the earliest indicator of relationships that will shatter. We haven't met other people's hopes for our relationships with them, and that has been hard. Some of it has been our fault. Julie and I overcommitted. We used to think that family makes promises and delivers big. When we did that, we hurt people.

(Julie)

The Bennetts Say the F-Word Too Much

We all want to be the hero in our own story, but sometimes the plotline is a bit more complicated than that. Take the storyline in the Bennett house of "having an open home." Since the beginning of our marriage, Chris and I have had an understanding that our house is meant to be place of connection and safety for others. Our first year of marriage was spent caring for a little boy named Michael, who was the son of my boss and friend. I babysat him, and he would often spend the weekend with us. I loved this boy, but as Chris and I have reflected on that time, we see that the choice to have Michael over for entire weekends proved that we didn't have healthy boundaries as a young married couple.

Our vision for creating a healthy family led to me trying to "rescue" lonely people, and over the years this rescue response ended up costing me so much precious time with my own family. It may have looked heroic on the outside, but it was detrimental on the inside. Have Chris and I had the best intentions in letting so many different people into our home? Of course! And did it make us feel good about ourselves? Yes, naturally. Did we pay attention to the warning signs that things were going badly in some of the situations that occurred in our "Bennetts' Bed and Breakfast" phase of twenty years? No.

In retrospect, we have come to realize that many of the people who lived with us over the years came with the overt need for a *home* but had a covert ask for a new *family*. There are a lot of ways to have someone outside your immediate family come live with you, and descriptors for the ones in our house spanned from "boarder" to "second son." While we should hesitate to call anyone our own child, especially at the onset of meeting them, Chris and I made a choice early on that if someone were going to live with us, we would treat them as one of us. We would call them an honorary Bennett.

Take Gisele, who had moved to Oklahoma from Brazil to work with the kids' programming at our church. She spoke wonderful English but was immediately confronted with the culture shock of living in a new country and culture.

Then there was Becky, who had a broken family life growing up—including abuse and abandonment—and was experiencing a healthy, although wild and crazy, family for the first time.

We also had my brother Greg live with us for a few months while he was engaged and waiting to get married. His six-foot-three frame had to curl up in the fetal position to fit on the couch each night. Pretty sure that couch carried his stench permanently, which is why we joyfully gave it away.

So besides the stinky couch, our free Airbnb life sounds magical and wonderful and Waltons-esque, doesn't it? Well, sometimes it was. We had many wonderful experiences and memories with each person. They were folded into our everyday lives without any fanfare, which was our goal. We wanted to make it all feel effortless and normal and real.

Take one of our housemates, Katrina, as an example. She often helped us tuck in our kids at night, read them bedtime stories, and pick them up after school. She went with us to Colorado for vacation and competed in our family talent show. She integrated into our lives beautifully and now acts as a big sister to all our kids.

But now we know that all our "big talk" caused some of those who came through our home collateral damage. Calling someone an "honorary Bennett" came, to them, with a lot of expectations. We didn't stop to consider that even if people are among your closest group of friends, there is still an order of care, and our physical family unit would take precedence. We continually fell short of their expectations and our own. They quietly got angry and sad and hurt, and in some cases, it was all unbeknownst to us until after they moved out. Those stories are the most painful ones.

Sometimes it was that we didn't understand what it meant to them to be an "honorary Bennett" or give them enough time to adjust to our rhythm and lifestyle. We hadn't recognized our own capacity for the love we had to give; we hadn't set boundaries. Chris and I pitched a vision of family that we never could live up to in a million years—we were spread thin as pastors and striving to be present and intentional parents to our children—and I see now how naive we were to think we could be everything to everyone.

No Such Thing As a Perfect Family

While all the "family" talk Chris and I dished out hurt us and those around us, what we all really suffered from was an overly idealistic image of what family can be. The "big talk" made it sound like once we brought people into our home, every part of our relationship was going to be about ease and comfort and care. That is just impossible. Family does not mean "easy." Call it what you want—idol, pot of gold, unicorn—but if the gleaming, golden image of the "perfect" family sits on a shelf in our minds, waiting to be found, we will live in loss and frustration. If we carry this unattainable ideal into our communities, our homes, or our friendships, nothing will stand up to it because in reality this holy grail does not exist.

"Perfect" ideals around family—what it can do and what it will give us—undergird so many of our reasons for walking away from relationships. Not only do we refuse to have clear and spoken expectations or goals in family relationships, but we also make the expectations that we do have totally unrealistic. But here's the best news—at least, it *feels* like the best news when we all sit around the table while our friends are fighting with us over what to do about politics in America and our kids are pushing each other for the last scoop of mashed potatoes:

There is no perfect family.

What a freaking relief, right? I bet you do what we do: watch other people with their dinner parties or Saturday morning walks and think, *Wow, they really have it all together. They're perfect.* It's the Instagram world that we live in—filters, shading, and multiple takes to get the perfect shot. This doesn't exist in real time in real life. Perfection is not the secret sauce to satisfying relationships; humanity is. Vulnerability is. The one thing we all have in common is that we're a mess.

When I was rushing to make it to an important meeting this past week, I saw a flashing digital sign informing me that the road I was on would be under construction for the next six months. *Six months?!* The completed construction will make the road smoother and the travel easier, but it creates havoc in the process. We all need big "Under Construction for Life" signs above our heads. Unless we not only expect people to change but actually allow it, we won't be able to maintain relationships with people as they grow.

One reason we know perfection isn't the glue that holds us together is just basic human math (human + human = human problems). I bring all of myself to every relationship, and even on my best days, I have a host of issues I'm working through and patterns of thought and behaviors I need to change. Even if the other person is basically Mother Teresa, the chance that my issues will clash with theirs is exponential. Our relationships with others are full of potential for connection and intimacy—and potential for disaster and miscommunication. In most family dynamics, both coexist.

How many holiday movies are based on a harmonious meal with no backstory of trauma where everyone feels so supported they can't stop smiling and eating the world's most succulent turkey? Oh right—none of them. The reason we all love watching holiday films is because they mirror us. We see ourselves in the overly controlling parent banging on the table to get the kids to stop fighting (even in their twenties); in the adults' ignorance to the child misbehaving in order to get attention; in the guest's reaction to the chaos, shell-shocked but still grateful to have been invited. Or maybe we are like Clark Griswold, trying to figure out how to get Cousin Eddie to move his "tenement on wheels" from the driveway and go home.[2] We relish when these not-perfect situations go haywire. Watching everyone bring the worst out of each other also leaves us laughing and realizing how those closest to us do the same. These films' plots unravel the pretending and perfectionism and reveal the love that reaches out into another's mess. Although family is a beautiful gift, it can't be neatly wrapped.

One day when Beau was around eight years old, Chris came down fairly hard on him for something he shouldn't have done. About fifteen minutes later, I came upstairs to find Beau frantically cleaning his room. I'd never seen that boy organize and properly put away things quite like he did that day. He looked up a bit sheepishly and said to me, "Mom, are you proud of me? Did I clean it right? Like you want?" My heart immediately broke. I called Chris upstairs, and we stopped him and pulled him close. We told him, "Son, you don't have to be perfect. You don't have to tidy everything up to prove to us you are good—to make up for what you did wrong."

The striving for perfection makes us do crazy things, especially in family. We must keep reminding each other that our love does not hang on one's performance. Just go watch *It's a Wonderful Life* and you will see. George Bailey nearly ended it all because he couldn't live up to his own standard of perfection.

And he learned in the end that although he wasn't perfect, the love of his friends and family was enough.

Perfection is a word that should be handled and used delicately. Does it exist? I would say no. (Unless you saw when my daughter walked in this morning to bring me a bracelet she made out of colored string. Now that was perfect!) But desiring perfection has been a hidden, sly little banner that has waved underneath most activities in my life. Thus it has popped up here and there in our family's life as well. No, you won't see "be perfect" on a mission statement in a business, a church, or my own kitchen chalkboard at home, but it is a felt standard. That's why we have to clarify the expectations we have around what *WTF* means to us.

(Chris)

In the children's book *Are You My Mother?* by P.D. Eastman, a mama bird is preparing for her baby to hatch, so she takes off to find some food. While she is gone, the little bird pops through the dainty shell and enters the world. He ends up tumbling to the ground from his nest. Unable to fly, the baby bird begins to walk around the foreign territory in desperate search for his mother. But he has never seen what his mother looks like, so he asks several animals as well as a boat, plane, and a tractor this question: "Are you my mother?"

It's hard to know what healthy family looks like when you've never had an example. Lots of people feel lost and disillusioned with what a healthy family is. I want to be clear: you don't have to grow up in a healthy family in order to experience it. It helps, but it's not necessary. Even healthy families inevitably have dysfunction. Why? Because where there are two or more humans, there are almost always two or more potential problems. Yet health is possible.

I have a close friend who grew up in a divorced home with adopted brothers who struggled most of their lives with drug and alcohol addiction. He was left playing the peacemaker and taking on responsibilities that someone his age should never have to take on. But he did it. And now that he has a family of his own, I have been amazed at the intentionality that he has poured into his wife and kids. Through lots of counseling and hard work, he has developed the once-atrophied muscles of connection. Building healthy family is possible.

Fighting for family—belonging to others and allowing them to belong to us—is a lifelong pursuit. We keep looking back at these watershed moments where a fresh wave of joy hits Julie and me about building belonging, and we learn something new. There's no one way to build families, and that's why it's such a rewarding pursuit. Just when you think you've got a system, you encounter new people, new places, even new pieces of yourself, and the whole thing has to change!

One of our dear friends gathers diverse groups of friends around the table so effortlessly (although I'm sure she's worked on it!), and each time, we take notes. On her fortieth birthday, she hosted a party at her house, cooked a three-course meal (caviar crudités to start), and then stood up to honor her guests one by one. The atmosphere was full of creativity and ease. She inspired us to keep making spaces where anyone can come to our table. There are infinite ways to create and build belonging.

(Julie)

Health and Hope

I've been going to a chiropractor this last year to help me with some back issues. Before she did a single treatment, she took X-rays and showed me where my spine was out of alignment. Once I could see what was wrong, I had no problem getting the proper adjustments.

Our hope is that in sharing our stories, we will help you see the misaligned expectations that need an adjustment in your own family so that the pain might ease a little. And once these expectations get realigned, it's amazing how things begin to fall in place.

We must stop the impossible pursuit of perfection and make the goal *health*. And in the words of Michael Jackson, "I'm starting with the man in the mirror."[3] That is, the beginning place in creating and sustaining a functional healthy family is *you*. Your personal responsibility to choose the journey of self-care, which really is about self-love. This can look like a variety of things but may include diet change, more sleep, less saying yes to everyone and everything, and therapy to work through trauma.

Here are some of our family goals we imperfectly practice:

- seeking to understand before needing to be understood, which we do by asking each other intentional questions

- believing the best of each other even when we are at our worst
- having open and honest conversations—no BS allowed
- working through hard things instead of walking away or shutting down
- inviting feedback without defense while giving space for the process

This road is messy but worth traveling. Some of you reading this have grown up in what you see as a wonderful, healthy family; you have had strong relationships with your parents and siblings and a stable home life. That is a wonderful gift. But that is not the norm for many Americans. By the age of eighteen, thirty, or fifty, many of us have experienced the pain of a divorce, dysfunction in the place that was supposed to be safe and consistent, abuse in the home, a sudden loss of friendship, or rejection by those closest to us. We all have expectations hiding behind the f-word, which means our own circumstances bring baggage into the conversation.

Cancer has shifted my perspective on everything, but mostly on people. When life is stripped down and you're simply trying not to die, it's the elemental things that matter. I simply wanted to be healthy—of heart, of body, of mind, and of soul. Cancer slowed me down so much I started aching not for a record-setting life but for deep, well-watered vitality. I recalibrated my focus and began to have healthy expectations of those around me. People didn't have to do so much to please me; they just needed not to be wildly dysfunctional! What a difference.

It's our dream that when you think of the f-word, you feel hope.

Hope that change and connection is possible.

Hope that it will be worth it.

We believe it is. We close our eyes, and the stories and memories pass by our minds, full of joy, pain, and laughter. At our core, our desire is to help those who have lost hope in family to find it again. To show them why we believe that community matters.

A few years ago, I was invited to join fourteen women every Thursday night here in Los Angeles. The invitation came from a woman named Sarah, who had initiated the gathering of these women from all different backgrounds. Sarah's support of our family was vital for us in our move to California. This group of women had been meeting for about two years, with no agenda other than to just be their true selves and share life with one another. When I got the invitation via text, I had a thrill of hope but then felt nauseous. Would it be worth it?

Yikes. Fourteen women? That commitment felt overwhelming and, considering my past experiences in a community of women, unsafe.

I finally accepted the invitation to the group the day I received my first cancer diagnosis in 2018. Chris thought I was a bit loony for wanting to go after receiving my diagnosis, but I did. I could've decided I didn't have the stamina to start new friendships, especially given the fact that I'd had enough bad experiences with female friendships to warn me off. But I stared down that mountain. I did a few jumping jacks, gave myself a little talk, tried to add some concealer to my teary and worn-out eyes, and cautiously showed up. I threw on my backpack full of fear and self-protection; grabbed my water, hiking shoes, and my tent just in case I needed to take cover; and I chose to try girl friendships again, hoping they would be the guides I needed this time around.

I was about to climb another mountain, this one called Cancer, and it was one I didn't want to do without a team. And these women, these Sherpas, whom I met as a group for the first time on diagnosis day? These women saved my life.

Our meetings always include a spread of delicious snacks and cheap wine selections, but that evening I didn't have my usual appetite for food. Instead, I hungered for someone to tell me I was going to make it. *Please*, I silently pleaded as I looked around the room, *tell me that moving to a new city with four kids, no home or job, and now cancer won't ruin us all.*

One hour in, after holding back as long as I could with fake half smiles and tired eyes, I broke. I blurted out, "My doctor called. My biopsy showed stage 3 cancer." The conversation stopped. During the brief silence, each woman was taking in this information in her own way. Then came the roar—a tribal roar of hope that I can feel in my bones today. They surrounded me and hovered over my body as if building some type of impenetrable force field. I still have the fifty-four-minute recording on my phone of promises, prayers, reminders, help, belief, and a space that held me. I truly believe this could not have happened anywhere else except in that living room. I didn't know how much I needed their sincerity until I was immersed in that moment.

In the darkest moments, in the stunning whiplash of the hard things, when we just want to retreat, is when being surrounded by friends and family is what we need the most. Life is a pilgrimage, at times requiring many companions.

I'm so thankful I chose not to stay home but to be held on that sacred, holy night. Over the next few years, these women—we call ourselves "GG" for "Girls Group"—walked me and my family through gift baskets, chemo treatments, meal plans, random smoothie runs, and sob fests where I didn't think I could give another inch. They gave me their inches.

I burst into tears every time that I think about that night. What made these stellar women such good guides on the journey were the uniqueness of their different voices, resounding like a patchwork quilt of wisdom, freedom, healthy expectations, and comfort all woven together. American, Australian, English, Southern, Northern, from the Midwest—there are a lot of lives represented in those voices. Yet all of them let me break—and I let myself break.

I didn't know safety existed quite like that until I experienced that night. We were open to one another. I didn't leave feeling insecure. I simply began to breathe again.

I'm not BFFs with all of them, and as the years have passed there are some I don't often see or hear from. But in some way we still belong to one another. The GG showed me an aspect of family that I desperately needed.

I learned to be loved in that family of fourteen diverse and loving women because they weren't trying to abide by a set of standards. And I would never use the word *perfect* about us, but definitely *sincere*. Their love was sincere. We bumped up against each other in ideology, politics, and personality differences. But when the climb got hard and the air a bit thin, we were ready to fight for relationship, to seek to understand and not just be understood. Because when love is sincere, it holds the power to transform. Perfect behavior doesn't form intimacy, but sincerity does.

You might be thinking, *This sounds like a lot. It doesn't sound real.*

You might be running the opposite direction of anything that looks, sounds, or hints of insincerity. We get that. But do you see that as humans, we can't help but always look for that sliver of relational hope, always try to reconnect again in some way?

In the last few years, we've seen the plantings of the desire for community breaking through what could've been the toughest ground: global, mandatory lockdowns during COVID-19. Do you recall the video that went viral of citizens in Italy early on in the pandemic? They were confined to their high-rise apartments yet flung open their windows and sang a ballad in solidarity.[4] It still gives me chills when I think about it. It was as if their voices were reaching out and embracing one another through song. It was an unbridled, sacred rejoinder of many together choosing hope and love.

The Road Map

Every adventure has a "hunt" attached to it. Like children who create a treasure map in an afternoon game or explorers seeking a fabled land of plenty, we are reluctant to set out on any risky adventure without a hope or a goal attached. If a band of people are going to stick together, they need a common goal—and families are no different. Chris and I have learned that once you start to walk through life with a person—whether because you exchanged vows with them or because you found each other playing Ultimate Frisbee at the park—you begin to have similar desires, from low-stakes ones like "have fun" to high-stakes goals like "expand our family." These are the markers of what your little group stands for, and it's important to say those values out loud. To have a mission statement, if you can handle the cringe-worthiness of such a thing. It's the starting line for the Bennett family and has been for a very long time.

For more than a decade, this family mission statement, intentionally written on our kitchen chalkboard, has stood the test of time: "We are a joyful family. We love Jesus, we serve each other, and we honor everyone."

Chris and I have recited this statement so many times with the kids—in a song, a rap, and a chant—that we usually have to stop midway through to tell them not to roll their eyes or say it in a robotic, monotone voice. That mission statement has served as a daily reminder (emphasis on *reminder*) of the kind of people we want to be and how we want to treat others as a result. It has offered us course correction when we get off track. Chris and I have never wanted to force our kids into certain behaviors, because doing so creates an environment of control. But while it looks great on a board, it can be unrecognizable in person.

Toward the close of summer 2020, we decided to break the mind-numbing monotony of the quarantine life and get away for a couple of days as a family. A few months prior, after celebrating nearly a year of cancer remission, we had received the news we had hoped never to hear again: my cancer had returned. I had been feeling a twinge and ignoring it. A knowing feeling had been clawing at my stomach. So I had spent spring 2020 undergoing unconventional cancer treatments in Spain, listening to the doctors' worst-case scenarios, and waiting for the results of various scans. All this was during the COVID-19 lockdown. It was so stifling. We were all struggling.

So that summer, we got out of town. We had days before we would receive the results of the latest scan to see whether my second round of treatments in Spain had worked, and the waiting was too hard. I wasn't yet ready to imagine the next steps (which would turn out to be two more different rounds of intense chemotherapy, more surgery, and then radiation treatments to boot).

In times of crisis, we can either isolate or we can grab our people and do some work. I get isolation, and I've done that. But let me tell you, grabbing our people? That's the right decision. Making choices about who you are going to be for each other, together, before the you-know-what hits the fan, is the move to make.

We packed the car up and drove to Big Bear, California—our mountaintop oasis. We went to the local grocery store and purchased large, white poster boards along with an assortment of Sharpies. Chris had told the kids beforehand that we were going to take time to remind ourselves of why we had uprooted our lives from Oklahoma. This felt particularly important because we needed our whole family to make the choice to stay in Los

Angeles again, no matter what was coming down the health pipeline.

On our first morning in Big Bear, it seemed like all the kids woke up on the wrong side of the bed. The sounds of sour attitudes quickly sent our hope for camaraderie into a nosedive almost as fast as the sugar crash from the mounds of syrupy pancakes they'd inhaled. So early in the day we paired up the kids to work on their relationships by having a scavenger hunt throughout the village. Over the years, when the kids have struggled with one another, we have tried to create fun through intentional planning sprinkled with wild, spontaneous moments of connection. Nothing fancy; just connection. For this adventure, each pair selected a team name, designed a poster and team chant, then ran around downtown following clues that led to the ice cream parlor, a vintage record store, a Jack-in-the-Box, and a few other places. We told them that the winning team would receive a cash prize. (Side note: it is amazing how quickly our children's desires to "connect" grow when money is involved.)

It was comical and memorable to say the least. At the end of the hunt, when the winner was announced, only one child broke down in tears. We considered that a win.

That evening after dinner, we partnered up the kids again to talk about our big fat reason *why*. Why are we in LA, and why should we stay? This activity is something our family has done at different times over the years when we were in a time of transition, prompted by changes such such as a move, new responsibilities, or new stages of life for our kids. We want to have a purpose for our family, and it can't just come from Mom and Dad. So we took turns throwing out reasons why we had come to LA and talking about the things we care about individually and as a family as we scribbled them on the sloppily taped poster board. We wanted to hold space for the kids to say anything that came to mind, without judgment, putting value on whoever was sharing without a debate, a laugh, or an eye roll. At one point, our son broke down in tears because all the kids wanted to do was leave LA. They had lost their why. Safety and unfiltered honesty helped our kids feel like their voices were heard. After multiple interruptions and some spirited conversations, we had our why: "We are here to love and serve the city of Los Angeles by creating inspiring media and building family."

We were still gathered around the rectangular walnut table at the cabin in Big Bear when I felt an overwhelming rumbling of emotions hit me like lightning. I was so uncertain of the impending results of my scans, and there were things I didn't want to leave unsaid. My heart burst open as I told each of the kids of the potential I saw in them. The reality of how short life really is was upon me. I felt like a hundred-pound weight was sitting on my shoulders. With tears flowing and snot bubbling, I began to speak words of life and purpose that I knew would be with them for the rest of their lives.

To my oldest son, I said, "Beau, you are a creative entrepreneur who will show others who they really are." I turned to Nate. "Nate, you are a powerful leader who will live out your dream to play quarterback in the NFL." Next I addressed Brooks: "Brooks, you are an entertainer with a heart of gold who will bring love and light wherever you go." And finally, to Joy: "Joy, you are a tender and strong woman with a voice that will be heard."

In that moment we felt the power and preciousness of this life we get to live as a family. Eleven-year-old Brooks swelled with a spiritual courage that Joan of Arc would have marveled at. With tears streaming and voice trembling, he burst out of his chair and passionately said, "Cancer ends with you, right here and right now, for you and our family. You will live a long and full life." There was so much power in his words as he berated this evil disease. If cancer could shake, it did. His faith stirred up a faith in all of us. Traces of fear were being evicted from our fidgety minds. We were given a burst of hope.

Something profound happens when everyone is given a voice. When everyone chooses solidarity. Does that inspire you? Even telling the story inspires us! When we remind one another that we have a joint mission that defines who we want to be, the space opens up for us to commit to each other again. Because we know our family motto, we are an *us*.

You can't find a perfect family, but you can become a healthy one. Building family is a process, and it doesn't happen overnight. It takes moments of overcoming misunderstanding and loss, and celebrating victories and joys. We've found it best to make the brave decision to fight for family before we face the incline of the family mountain. To resolve to stick with it and not be easily scared off. With that decision made, we know that choosing to pursue living life with other people will be worth it in the end, no matter how many times we shout or mutter "WTF?" along the climb.

So think about your own tribe, your crew, your people—whatever you want to call it. Each person you're in relationship with is uniquely wired. But agreeing on a statement—whether you call it that or something less formal—honors the differences and brings a unity that keeps each member connected. A shared mission gives a deeper purpose to the relationship, helps to eliminate unrealistic expectations, and aligns the right expectations.

Write Your Mission Statement

We invite you to write your own family mission state-ment. It can be intensely intimate or fun and silly. Gather with your kids, roommates, or even closest friends, and openly discuss what you care about. What do you value? Those values can be curated into a statement of purpose, or mission, that serves as a guidepost in how you relate to each other.

This exercise may feel too formal for some of you; that's OK. But it is a helpful exercise to define what matters to you most, as this will greatly impact the relationships that you hope to build.

Chapter 3

Table of Honor

Fellowship is a kind of belonging that isn't based on status, achievement, or gender, but instead is based on a deep belief that everyone matters, everyone is welcome, and everyone is loved, no conditions, no exceptions.
—BRIAN D. MCLAREN, *WE MAKE THE ROAD BY WALKING*

(Julie)

Goldie

Most of you have probably never visited an elementary school assembly only to see a five-foot-six-and-a-half-inch-tall (to be exact) middle-aged woman dressed in gold yelling joyfully at all the kids about how awesome they are. But if you had come to our youngest kid's school, you just might have.

It was 2014 at Monroe Elementary in Norman, Oklahoma, where I first introduced my alter ego, Goldie, to four hundred wild and crazy elementary students. Goldie dresses from head to toe in gold spandex, wears a purple wig (or whatever wig is currently calling to me from my closet), and finds immense joy in watching the students come alive when I hand out plastic gold coins that come with the reminder that they are worth more than gold.

The most epic moment was the Friday morning that I showed up in my costume and surprised every student with their own personalized gold cape. The back touted the phrase "We can all be heroes!" Based on their reaction, you would have thought they'd just won a trip to Walt Disney World. To add to the excitement, I had bribed Beau, who was in sixth grade, with an Egg McMuffin to dress up in an undersized Buzz Lightyear costume. The rest of that day the coolest thing began to happen. These little kids gave out their own gold coins to other kids, and even their parents at home, to tell them how awesome they were.

Goldie's visit wasn't meant to be a gimmick or a "sticker moment"—something slapped on that falls off the next day. It was about planting seeds in these little hearts that would one day grow. It was about "calling out the gold"—the special skill or quality in each child—and saying, "I see you." "Honor is for everyone" is not just a neat idea but an essential concept we need in order to thrive.

Calling out the gold in other people never stops. We don't grow out of it, and we don't arrive at a payday. We just keep the coins moving. Kindness is contagious.

Are your relationships full of gold—moments where treasure is being "discovered" in one another?

Our Tabletop (or) the Centerpiece

In our home, honor is the table we lay everything else on top of. You know when someone says, "You honor me with your presence"? That's what we Bennetts want our lives to say to each and every person.

Chris and I have seen firsthand how honor opens up our ability to see and hear the people in front of us and to bring sincere appreciation for their personhood in our time together. We welcome people to bring their full selves, however they are. It's not an easy way of living, but it's stable.

As a kid, I used to love watching the TV show *Cheers*. Nearly every scene during its eleven-season run took place in a bar named Cheers on Beacon Hill in Boston, Massachusetts. The show portrayed a handful of characters who were all "formers"—former baseball player, accountant, actor, and fiancée. For various reasons, they had all found themselves at Cheers either bussing tables, filling up frosted mugs, or making themselves at home at the mahogany bar along with other customers. The bar built a reputation that no matter who you were or where you came from, this was a place "where everybody knows your name, and they're always glad you came."[1]

Wouldn't we all love to find a place like that? These spaces seem rare. I bet that rather than a litany of memories that compare to the Cheers bar, more of us are familiar with the opposite kind of story: moments when we felt unseen and dishonored.

I had to switch schools midyear during sixth grade, and I can still feel the knots in my stomach when I remember walking into the cafeteria for lunch on my first day, not a familiar face in sight. I cringe thinking about that helpless feeling and the loud, crowded cafeteria filled with cliques and the overwhelming smell of microwaved meatloaf. I had just finished reading a mean letter someone shoved through the cracks in my locker that read,

"You're not that pretty, your nose is big, and go back to where you came from!" I held back my tears so I wouldn't get shunned any further as I moseyed my way to an empty chair. Guess I would be eating my PB&J by myself.

Life can often feel like that overcrowded cafeteria. We all have felt like we aren't wanted, aren't seen, or don't belong. It can appear that everyone has a reserved seat except for us. *Why doesn't anyone want me at their table? Does anyone even see that I am looking for a place to sit?* "Get in where you fit in" sounds great as a tagline, but even for us adults it can seem like there are no tables with empty seats in sight.

We live in a world that tends to propagate the insignificance of others. News and social media are littered with people's dirt, and society can't seem to get enough of it. It's as if the world is watching and waiting for others to fail. We need voices reminding us who we really are and helping us make choices that bring us toward who we want to be. Our bodies, our minds, our personalities—they are glorious. Chris and I believe that every person alive bears the image of God—we hold glory—in our faces, our lives, and our very beings.

(Chris)

The Stories That We Tell

The stories that we tell each other matter. From the moment someone enters your life, you have the opportunity to open doors for them, roll out the red carpet, and go all in on reminding them that they have something nobody else has. It's a narrative chock-full of sincerity and the "good stuff." To the question lingering in each of our minds—*Am I someone special?*—we can answer for you with an exuberant "Yes!" We tell our kids that everyone is a child of God, and that they must rise up and become people who look into the eyes of others and tell them what they see: magic.

Practically, honor can't be just something we think about. It must be *practiced*, and sometimes that practice can feel awkward. One of our favorite things to do around the table with a first-time guest is to play "hot seat," where the guest is put on the spot to answer a handful of lighthearted questions from our family as quickly as they can. We have found that even introverts love the game. We each have our go-to questions. For a long time now, Joy has led with "What's your favorite movie?" followed by "Who's your favorite Disney princess?" Nate will tend to lean toward a sports-related question, and Brooks will ask whom out of anyone in the world you would want to have dinner with. Julie tends to lead with the deep question "What's your favorite ice cream?" I always ask, "If you could have a private concert in your living room with a deceased musician, who would it be?" (Beau and I would, hands down, pick Frank Sinatra.) These questions are meant to put our guests at ease, and we love hearing their answers. It's a creative way to get to know them better—the first step of building family.

Just to be clear, *honor* shouldn't be confused with *flattery*. It's not a "I have to" but an unforced, un-manipulative gift we give to those around us. It may take effort, but ease and love should be the anchor of our honor—without needing anything in return.

So what are the ingredients that make up honor? We can start here: honor sees everyone at the table. There are no invisible guests.

(Julie)

Everybody Gets a Turn

Home is often the hardest place to practice showing honor, but we need it here the most. Whether we're dealing with a spouse, a child, or a roommate, we each get a front-row seat to one another's imperfections and quirks. Most people look really good from a distance or in an Instagram post, but up close and personal, our flaws and blemishes are unavoidable and unfiltered. Honoring someone at their worst can be an immense challenge, so it's important to establish practices that keep honor at the forefront of our relationships.

One of our family's practices is making certain that each person receives ample celebration. To set a "table of honor," we must reject hierarchy and the horrible habit of celebrating only those in positions of power. It can't be that every gathering or text chain is about one person's high-paying career, constant interactions with famous people, or pulling the best-looking dates. A table where one person constantly gets the spotlight and everyone else is left in the shadows is just asking for a huge family blowup.

Honor means meeting each person where they are at. A child

is celebrated for sharing their lunch with a classmate or being kind to the new kid at school. A teenager is high-fived (do they even let us do that anymore?) or you "dap them up" for getting their learner's permit. A person in recovery is hugged extra long for just showing up. You see what we mean? In this theater, there is no spotlight, no place where characters disappear into the background. The stage has lights everywhere, coming up out of the floors.

Do you know something I love about us Bennetts? We *do* birthdays. I mean, *we do them.* We fill up the kitchen and bedrooms with balloons, drape our reusable Happy Birthday banner across the kitchen window, and sneak in a confetti popper somewhere along the way. We make the person's favorite breakfast. (Don't be impressed. This is usually my children's excuse to eat Pillsbury cinnamon rolls.). We take them to an awesome lunch, and then Chris usually makes sous vide steaks for dinner. While eating, we go around the table and tell the birthday boy or birthday girl why they are so awesome.

Maybe you are rolling your eyes right now and thinking, *My family and friends would never do that.* But I happen to know you're wrong. I've seen it done in many settings with lots of different types of people.

There's something so intimate that happens around the dining table. I love our living room, where we pile in shoulder to shoulder to watch a movie or play a game, but often our deepest connections and most meaningful conversations happen at the table. Everyone tends to be more engaged, more present, and more of a contributor.

Last week I substituted in Nate's high school history class, and the kids mentioned it was a classmate named Ethan's birthday. They had a worksheet to get done, but we stopped for a few minutes and I asked the kids to share what made Ethan so valuable. I was nervous it might go down like a rat sandwich, but right away one student raised a hand, followed by another. Even high school kids aren't too cool for this. Nate chimed in that Ethan was the one who made him feel the most welcome on his first day of seventh grade after we moved to LA. I watched Ethan's cheeks get red and saw these kids' hearts find so much joy in making him feel special. (Um, and I might have made them all pound on their desks while I did a birthday rap. Poor Nate.)

The dam of hesitancy broke, and honor overtook the room.

(Chris)

The Round Table

Here's a second guideline for showing honor in our relationships: our tables must have a seat for *everyone*, regardless of status. When honor is strong, and the legs of the table we sit at are made of sturdy stuff, we can lay just about anything on top of it.

The actual tables in everyone's homes, offices, and churches may be rectangular or oval or what have you, but the metaphorical "family table" is a round one. There is no head of the table in relationships, just a shoulder-to-shoulder, round surface with room for all—like King Arthur's Round Table. We must have a space where each member is an equal, regardless of whether they are royalty or a minor player. In a nuclear family, we can't ignore the input of those younger than us or those we may think have less to contribute. That distinction doesn't exist. Opening space for children and youth to participate isn't just good for them; it's good for us. We all grow. But building equality into our culture so that everyone has a voice takes a high level of intentionality.

Julie and I look to Jesus' life for examples of living with intentionality and making space for all at the table. Contrary to what some of us might have experienced, true religion—a love-filled practice of life—refuses status worship. Jesus told his followers that when they attend a banquet, they should take the lowest seat at the table instead of jockeying for the seat of honor (Luke 14:7–11). A letter to early Christians later attributed to James, Jesus' brother, instructed readers not to show partiality toward those with higher status: "Suppose a man comes into your meeting wearing a gold ring and fine clothes, and a poor man in filthy old clothes also comes in. If you show special attention to the man wearing fine clothes and say, 'Here's a good seat for you,' but say to the poor man, 'You stand there' or 'Sit on the floor by my feet,' have you not discriminated among yourselves and become judges with evil thoughts?" (James 2:2–4). We could not agree more with that sentiment.

Meet the Avis Family

Our good friends Josh and Heather Avis run a nonprofit called The Lucky Few Foundation, which is a social awareness campaign on a mission to create a more inclusive world, emphasizing shifting the current Down syndrome narrative that tends to question the worth and value of this amazing community of people.[2]

Both Josh and Heather have taught us so much about the worth and value that everyone carries, especially those with Down syndrome. Just being around them has taught us how to be courageous advocates for those who have been overlooked or marginalized by society. After years of infertility, they adopted three kids, two of whom have Down syndrome. Through their social awareness initiative, book writing, seminars, and podcast, Josh and Heather are teaching others how to see and honor the worth in others regardless of who they are or what they look like. When we sat down for an interview with the Avises back in January 2020, Josh said it so well: "The issue isn't that they have Down syndrome; it's how the world views their Down syndrome."

When their daughter with Down syndrome, Macy, was not going to be allowed in a regular classroom with her peers, Heather kindly but firmly met with the school leadership to challenge their decision and bring understanding. The school changed their position, and Macy jumped right in. Heather fights for inclusion for her kids, but she also helps others see how inclusion benefits everyone, not just those receiving a seat at the table. We have watched them up close as they have devoted themselves to pointing out the worth and value of every human. We have watched them fight for family again and again. They have a slogan for themselves: "Shouter of worth." What an awesome goal. We must shout the worth and value of others louder than the destructive voices that seek to tear people down.

Meet Lambert Lo

Over the last few years, we have developed a friendship with an inspiring guy named Lambert Lo. Several years ago, he felt moved to serve the overlooked and often undervalued homeless community. While serving on staff at a local church, he made a decision to reserve the front row of the sanctuary for the homeless men and women who camped in front of the church property on Sunday mornings. Instead of dismissing them, he created a seat for them. As you may expect, not every parishioner was a fan of this gesture, but Lambert didn't stop there. He now hosts a monthly gathering called the King's Table where a host opens their home and serves a five-course dinner prepared by a top-rated chef. The special guests are those experiencing homelessness.

Our family had the privilege of serving at one of the gatherings just before the pandemic shut things down. I sat by Justin, a man who played eleven musical instruments, and he shared his story with me. He had had a wife and a good job but suffered from debilitating seizures that would take out years of his memory. In a series of unfortunate events, his wife left him, he lost his job, and then he became homeless. But then he found these gatherings, where he felt connection and honor. Slowly, over time and many shared meals, he began to believe in family again, though it looked much different than it used to. Justin went from hopeless to hopeful.

The peace he had as he spoke amazed us—each word held no trace of bitterness. As I listened to his heartbreaking story, I realized how many judgments I have had made about people experiencing homelessness. Not every person in those circumstances is there because of a bad decision or laziness. Unexpected, unfair events can place us in dire situations. We do not get what we deserve, because life doesn't work like that.

On the drive home, my daughter said something that was more profound than she realized: "I couldn't tell who was homeless and who wasn't." *That's* the power of a round table. It creates equality. There is no better place to share humanity than around a meal.

Fellowship is for scarred people and for scared people, and for people who want to believe but aren't sure what or how to believe. In his bestselling book *Tribe: On Homecoming and Belonging*, Sebastian Junger shares a powerful quote from Rachel Yehuda, who works with traumatized vets: "If you want to make a society work, then you don't keep underscoring the places where you're different—you underscore your shared humanity."[3] When we come together just as we are, with honor, we begin to rise again, to believe again, to hope again, to live again.

(Julie)

What Honor Ain't

Chris and I have spent a lot of time in the South, so let's be clear: honor ain't blowing smoke up someone's . . . It's not nonstop compliments or flattery. It shouldn't require demeaning yourself or someone else. It's not based on comparison. It shouldn't make anyone else feel not-enough. Honor is when we give out of sincerity and expect nothing in return. Honor elevates the status of others because we believe they are worth it.

In many homes and families, the language of honor has been used as a smoke screen for broken and even abusive relationships and patterns. We do not endorse this. It is unacceptable for any person to leverage their position in order to take advantage of others and then use "honor" as a cover-all. True respect cannot be demanded, because it is based upon love, not fear. If you ever meet a person who *demands* loyalty from you, we hope you run the other way. It is only a matter of time before you will find yourself on the receiving end of control tactics, and that's no place any of us want to be.

Empty flattery is just as destructive; it does not breed trust or intimacy. We've all been there—you try to express a frustration or confess how you're failing at something but you are summarily dismissed. Maybe you share with a friend that you are struggling to connect with your teenager. You feel the distance between you and your child, and you don't know what you're doing wrong. You're being vulnerable with your friend, acknowledging that you've missed the mark and need to get it off your chest. But your friend responds to your honesty and pain by saying, "Oh, I don't think it's as bad as that. You're such an amazing parent."

Womp, womp. Yes, maybe that's true. And I'm sure your friend believes they're honoring you. But we don't build intimacy by pretending others are perfect, right? We need a safe space where we can work through conflict, share honestly, or even achieve person-to-person reconciliation. We must view others as sacred and see the failure, the confession, and the continual transformation as something to be held with great reverence. We don't erase the beauty of someone else's humanity. For our lives to be a place of total release and safety for one another, we have to know that we are really seen—with all our issues—and celebrated anyway.

Imagine the Possible

Let's imagine the toasting of a misty-eyed, esteemed group of people who feel welcome to gather at any meal. A literal place where they are free to be themselves—to learn, to listen, to receive, to disagree or agree, to celebrate, to grieve, to just be.

What if?

That space must be made without the qualification of being rich or poor. It must not only have joyful curiosity but harbor no expectations based on one's background or skin color, gender or agenda.

Right before COVID-19 hit, we were sitting around our dining room table with some friends. I watched as Chris and our friend Caleb were trying to say the same thing but in completely different ways. Chris realized that some of the language he used—coming from Oklahoma and a pastoral background—didn't make sense in a city like Los Angeles. And as we passed around the food and drank our wine, Chris and I discovered that we were learning a new language—one that didn't depend on us having the answers for the people around us. We weren't the only hosts. We were all hosting each other and learning from one another's cultures and vocabularies. As the night went on and our candelabra held the dim light of our drippy, eight, uneven white candles, our hearts connected in a deep, deep way.

Now that's what we are in this for: to rest, to share, to commune over the common and the different. Allowing people to come into our home as they are helps us to shift narratives, refine our methods, and smooth out the rough edges of our convictions.

Like we said earlier, language matters. Our favorite definition of *honor* comes from Bill Johnson: "celebrating who a person is without stumbling over who they are not." We are convinced that every human being on the planet was created by God with beauty and goodness woven into the fiber of their soul.

The Practice

To be honest, our family dinners can feel forced at times, but we know the value of them. So we have a few rules that help them along:

Rule One: No one is allowed to bring any type of device to the table.

Rule Two: We make space to talk about our days—the good and the bad.

Rule Three: We practice listening with our eyes, resisting the urge to interrupt.

Rule Three is particularly challenging. I find myself asking my kids, "Are you hearing me?" five hundred times a day. For me, feeling like people aren't listening is the worst. My kids hear most everything that Chris and I ask of them or share with them (as long as there isn't a device in their hands), but we have realized that just because they are *hearing* our words doesn't mean they are *listening*. We want to create a lifestyle of honoring the voices of others, starting in our own nuclear family.

Listening is a discipline that leads to empathy. Kelly Workman, a psychologist at Columbia University Medical Center, explained that "hearing is the passive intake of sound while listening is the act of intentionally working to comprehend the sounds you hear."[4]

Our family has decided to practice not having phones in pockets when in our house, or on our persons while watching a movie. We put them on Airplane mode when we are doing anything that doesn't require Wi-Fi.

You might wonder what texting has to do with honor, but I promise—there's an important point here. Nobody can ignore that the digital age has had an effect on our ability to connect. Chris and I have taught our kids to listen with their expressions, with their whole bodies, when someone is talking. Yet we learned recently that when our kids say that they were "talking" to their friend, this means that they either texted or, most likely, sent a "Snap" to them through Snapchat (had to google that one). It may sound old school, but to us, "talking" requires verbal communication. You can't feel real tears or taste the salt of another, if you will, on an app that deletes messages within seconds. Talk about disconnected. My concern is that there is an entire generation whose emotional development is stunted in large part due to their addiction and reliance upon screens for communication.

As parents, we know there is a lot of talk about our kids and their phones. We've all tried talking, screaming, threatening, or throwing in the towel over how addicted they are and what to do about it. Pew Research Center's recent survey found that 95 percent of teenagers report having a smartphone.[5] And while scientists disagree on whether excessive smartphone use can be considered an addiction, they do agree that "overuse is detrimental to a person's mental health."[6] And it's not just teenagers; adults, too, can check their smartphones compulsively.

I was at lunch with someone recently, and they kept their hand on their phone almost the whole lunch. I could see the disconnect in their eyes. Then I was at coffee with a friend last week, and I chose to leave my phone on the table instead of in my purse. I quite literally could not stay present in the conversation just because my phone was beside me. In our opinion, this culturally accepted practice is steeped in dishonor; it values our devices more than the person in front of us.

I've had a front-row seat to an expert listener: my husband, Chris. Ask anyone who has known him more than a minute and they'll tell you the same thing. He honors others with his ability to be present through active listening. That might look like refusing to be distracted, giving constant eye contact, or having relaxed and open body language that makes me feel at ease and valued in the moment. It's so worth it to pay attention to that person in your life who is modeling active listening, like I have (mostly) with Chris. Oh, how I need this man. I've recently celebrated the intentional shift in myself toward being more present. Suffering forced that on me. It caused me to slow down and appreciate the present moment in a way I hadn't allowed myself before.

Active listening and being present is full of honor. It is a way of saying, "This moment has value. The people in it have value. I am not leaving the now for the what-if."

(Chris)

Hosting One Another

The ultimate goal of being seated at a table of honor is for our time together to be a place of rest from pretending and thinking only of ourselves. When we feel heard, we breathe a little easier. We steward—we cultivate—our communication, what we share and think as we look into the eyes of those in the room. The experience transforms us. When we feel that there is *space* for us, our whole selves—not just the parts we have shared—feel seen.

Just this week, some kids at school were making fun of Brooks for being the only one in his grade who didn't have an iPhone yet—so they called him "iPad boy." Clever kids, very original. Now typically we'd just say, "No biggie, Brooks. Let that roll off your back. It could be worse, buddy." But it was a big deal for him, and because of the teasing he was feeling ostracized, a bit like an outsider. So that evening while eating our weekly dose of grilled chicken and veggies (except Nate—please, someone help him like vegetables), Brooks was in the spotlight. His siblings reminded him what they celebrate about him. After that night, he wrote some thoughts and emotions he wanted to share with Julie and me about the phone, and so much more. It was such a tender process.

Honor validates everyone and refuses to minimize the real pain and emotions that others are carrying. This doesn't mean there aren't times where we step in to give correction, offer a different perspective, or provide counsel, but we have to earn these things over time by gaining relational equity.

Brooks felt free to share the raw emotions in his heart and felt safe enough to invite us into that space with him. He said, "I know I shouldn't care, but I do." Julie and I could hear and see the shame he felt. We told him it was OK to care and to feel; it wasn't wrong.

As parents, we make the decisions that we believe are best for our children. But Julie and I have learned (and keep learning) that valuing the voice of your children (or anyone else, for that matter) and empowering them really matters. If we didn't create that space for Brooks to share and acknowledge that his feelings were valid, the subtle message of "you don't belong with us; you don't fit in" could become a splinter in his heart that he could carry for many years to come.

Cultivating Dignity

You're probably picking up on the fact that that honor is the centerpiece of our family culture. It is one that takes time and intentionality. It's about building something every day that will pay off, but likely in invisible, intangible ways. And yes, that can be hard.

We've been trying to grow grass in our yard, and it's been an excruciating experience. A friend told us, "Just throw some seed and scatter it on top of what you already have, water it once

a day, and *boom*! You'll see new grass in a couple of weeks."
Easy-peasy. Well, two weeks passed, and nothing sprouted. So
we looped back to step one. I borrowed our neighbor's tiller, and
my son and I spent hours breaking up the ground. We scattered
more seed, laid some soil on top of the bare places, and watered
regularly—but as I'm writing this, we are still waiting on growth.

Forming honor is a lot like this process. We can throw seed
around, but we may never see anything resembling a lawn.
Choosing to build all your communal time with the superpower of
honor is not a flippant decision. It's sincere and takes time. We can't
control the external circumstances that inhibit growth, but we can
control the intentional work that we put into the hard ground.

Cultivating dignity—building a whole life undergirded by
principles of listening to, receiving, and honoring others—is a
never-ending journey. It's like creating a landscape from scratch.
Like a watchful gardener, you'll never stop tending and being
amazed at the growth.

Our family is learning how to hold space for ourselves more
than ever these days, at meals and at our one-on-one date nights
with each other. In those moments, the roots go deeper. Julie and
I have learned, as we practice these virtues, that we can make
the choice to show honor over and over again. Breathe in honor.
Breathe out honor.

You are probably familiar with the phrase "familiarity breeds
contempt" from *Aesop's Fables*. If honor is about valuing, then
contempt is about devaluing. The more familiar we become
with someone—whether it's a spouse, child, coworker, team-
mate, or friend—the more intentional we must be to maintain

honor in the relationship. How many relationships have become so comfortable that we have forgotten the gold we saw at the beginning?

Every person is created with inherent worth and value. As time goes on, disappointments happen, and the dirt of life can begin to bury the gold (or gifts) we each have to offer. But when we aren't distracted or discouraged by people's jagged edges, and we dig with our pickaxes until we discover that little fleck of gold, we can find treasure. And when we do, we celebrate it.

We have the ability to awaken others by seeing them for who they are and calling forth that which they might have thought was lost. We are each worth what honor can give us, and we can all help to build an oversized, sturdy place of honor for others to sit around. Soon enough, those people will become family.

Work the Muscle

This week, think about how you can "call out the gold" in someone from your home, work, or neighborhood. Share with that person what you value about them.

Or throw an "honor dinner" in which you invite a few friends or neighbors to celebrate everyone around the table. Assign each person an honor recipient as they walk in the door, or write a list of adjectives on a board and let people choose which one they want to give to the person seated on their left.

Most of all, though, take time to look everyone you are speaking to in the eye, and make a point to put your phone in your pocket or bag as soon as you begin a conversation. See what honoring others with active listening feels like.

Chapter 4

Excuse the Mess

I always thought that the "thriving" would come when everything was perfect, and what I learned is that it's actually down in the mess that things get good.
—JOANNA GAINES, *THE MAGNOLIA STORY*

(Julie)

Why This Mess Is Blessed

I admit it; Chris and I need help. Occasionally, we will spend the money to have someone clean our house. It's not the scrubbing or vacuuming that takes it out of us but the 101-plus times I bend over to pluck a sock, a wrapper, a paper, or a LEGO off the floor and put it back in its original home. I can't properly explain the euphoria and peace of coming home to a freshly mopped floor and lemon zest in the air. It's miraculous; yet it doesn't last for long. With four kids, a dog, and a husband, my tranquil and tidy house reverts back to its previous condition quickly. So I have learned that if I want to enjoy my time inside my house—and live in it with thankfulness—I need to appreciate my home despite its disarray.

Do you know the phrase "We can't see the forest for the trees"? Well, Chris and I have discovered that sometimes we can't see the family for the mess. The bad habits, the little interruptions, the full-on meltdowns people bring into our days can cloud our vision. If we choose to have people in our lives, some litter is not only unavoidable; it's necessary.

Both of us are always on our kids to pick up behind themselves, but I'm the loudest. An incessant voice, so constant that Chris often taps my shoulder to ease up, because while we don't want irresponsible kids, this cannot be a ceaseless chorus they hear. There are other things that need to be said. Sometimes we need to let the issue go. If we have to tidy everything before we feel at rest, we aren't fully healthy. I call that voice in my head "Crazy Lady Who Needs Control." She doesn't need to be there, but she's the outcome of something that has zero to do with cleanliness.

To counter her and keep her at bay, I frequently remind myself that someday I'll miss yelling up the stairs to my teenage boys to pick up their one hundred pairs of shoes strung out all over the house. Someday, I'll no longer have to overlook the ridiculous amount of gum wrappers and chip bags that I can find in sheets or under a bed.

I saw a quote the other day that hit home, especially with a couple of teenagers who are headed out of our house and into the world quicker than I'd like. It said: "If you think their messy room is hard to look at, just wait until it's empty." As much as I complain and sigh, finding those gum wrappers or a random shoe without its mate can make me smile. I imagine which child left it behind and what they were doing when it happened. All these things are the telltale signs of a house lived in. A home full of people.

Clean Is Boring

Think about a close friend, partner, sibling, or family member. Imagine erasing any memory or conversation that was hard, tense, inconvenient, or challenging. Imagine that you were identical to each other, so you never pushed each other to think outside the box because you didn't realize you needed to. Wouldn't you feel like something was off? We weren't designed for dull, robotic relationships that stay the same day after day. How *boring*, right? And not just boring but depressing and lifeless. We weren't made to keep our relationships like we would our homes when guests are on their way—picked up, dusted off, and spotless.

Here are three ideas—three commitments, really—that can reign in our control and perfection impulses. Let me tell you, these are hard but worth it. And they keep us alive in our relationships. Try saying them aloud as you are reading.

1. I admit that I can't control everything.
2. I will be messy around others.
3. I will let other people be complicated.

Oh, friend, this is what Chris and I have painfully learned: control and performance never bring the validation we long for. They don't build family.

(Chris)

Food Fights and Family Hangs

Have you seen *Hook*, the reimagining of the classic Peter Pan story from the perspective of a grown-up Pan? Robin Williams plays a Pan who has grown up and forgotten all of his "Lost Boy" instincts, including how to fly. The pivotal change for him comes when he is seated at a table and every boy is eating what appears to Pan to be imaginary food. Williams's character gets so caught up in a verbal mud-slinging fight with Rufio, the new head of the Lost Boys, that in the midst of triumph, Pan pulls back his spoon and flings "pudding" at Rufio. As soon as it hits, Pan's eyes are truly opened to the table. It's filled with delectable morsels, sumptuous meats, and multicolored desserts. The boys start to throw colorful globs of sugary mousse at each other, and everyone is laughing and free. It's what releases Pan to find his magic again.[1]

It's hard to enjoy people if you can't play. And you can't play without getting dirty.

When Julie and I first started dating, we worked with a ragtag group of youth in Lorena, Texas. You want to talk about messy? We met in an old asbestos-filled middle school that smelled like you might imagine (if you imagine a mix of urine, mildew, rat droppings, and failed attempts of Febreze to cover it up). We converted the cafeteria into our youth center, which contained donated Ping-Pong tables, a pool table, and a dusty basketball court. Without fail, each week we would have some of the most troubled kids in the area show up, like a kid named Parker who

84

lived in a nearby trailer home. I'll never forget dropping him off after youth group one night and seeing hundreds of cockroaches scurrying throughout the house.

We would sing a few songs during each service, and Parker would sit on the front row (sometimes standing on top of a chair) and perform his best rendition of a Backstreet Boys dance that he had learned. It was awkwardly sweet. Our gatherings were the one place he felt that he could be himself, as he was often bullied at school and was neglected at home. We have stayed in touch with him, and he is now married with a family and employed as a fire juggler. No joke and no surprise.

Then there was Jason, who, along with a few of his pothead buddies, would straggle in on Wednesday nights. Pretty sure they didn't come for the spiritual experience, but we wanted to show them that "There's no high like the most high God." (OK, bad joke.) Julie would tell them to put out their joints before they came into the building. They would reluctantly oblige and beg her not to tell me about it. I guess that, of the two of us, I was the enforcer. They were afraid of being kicked out; they wanted to be there because they knew they would be loved.

I will never forget Jimmy, who had slurred speech and some issues at school. He came every week. If you could get a gold star for attendance, Jimmy would have gotten it. He would call our house multiple times a day and leave us the same voicemail, word for word, on our answering machine. I still remember the exact message: "Chris, this is Jimmy. Give me a call, or don't give me a call. Bye." He taught us so much about contentment and the pure joy of being together.

Looking back, Julie and I can see that it was always in our DNA to take in the outcasts, the misfits, and the square pegs who never quite fit in the round hole. It gritty work that taught us to look past a person's exterior.

Those years at the old middle school in Lorena shaped how we would do life moving forward. We realized that we needed them as much as they needed us. Making the choice to allow people to come "as they are" and not "as they should be" set us up for later success, but those choices didn't come cheap. "Dirty people are welcome" sounds so gracious until they sit on our white sofa. If you have a white sofa (proverbial or literal), maybe you can benefit from the same pep talk we give ourselves. You bought the sofa (drumroll) to be sat on!

Remember those commitments we shared earlier? Say it with us: We can't organize our friends. We won't control our family. Even if it takes one hundred thousand pep talks, we will loosen our grips and know that *mess* is a sign of freedom.

(Julie)

People Aren't Things: Letting Other People Be Complicated

Organization-focused shows like *Tidying Up with Marie Kondo* and *Get Organized with the Home Edit* have swept through the nation. We all love the idea of making our lives as simple, clear, and "joy sparking" as possible. And while we can't and likely shouldn't get rid of people as easily as Kondo dismisses a never-worn sweater. If we threw out relationships that were complicated in favor of relationships that were simple, we'd be left with an empty room. This ordered control can make us feel safe, but it's a false sense of safety. It's lonely.

Does the fact that you can't control your environment make you feel a tiny bit anxious? We think that's pretty normal. But it's also important to manage if you want to be close to other people. To be clear, you get to make choices about what kinds of interruptions and problems you can handle; that's a part of making your house yours. But you can tell when saying no to having other people in your life is a pattern rather than an exception. A pattern that perhaps uses a need for perfection to avoid intimacy. Often, this can be a form of self-protection to ward off rejection. This behavior might be stopping you from building the life you most want.

Mess can unhinge us and unravel our composure. At times, I've wondered who will win—Control Cleaning Lady or Best Friend Julie. But allowing disorder is essential to building relationships. If we communicate through our words or actions that issues are not allowed, it won't take long before people stop coming around. Because *everyone is a mess*. Sure, some clean up better than others and some are more self-aware than others, but everyone has some trash, some laundry left on the floor.

It's hard—practically impossible—to create a relaxing environment when someone is always trying to dictate what's going on. Chris and I know this, but it does not mean we've mastered the art of letting go. I am still learning to give space for my kids to have a hard day, be grumpy, and work it out in their time.

My parenting style does not involve a poker face. I sigh. I shake my head and say things that sound like someone lit my mouth on fire. I am intense at the wrong moments. And this has caused my kids to close off in some of their most vulnerable moments because what they needed was my gentleness.

Just this week I've felt such a deep irritation toward Chris and the kids because I've been unable to self-regulate during some family stress. *Self-regulation* is getting yourself into a space where you aren't running hot or cold; it's taking deep breaths and practicing mindfulness when things get rough.

After our chaotic first six months in LA, which included twenty moves around the city, we at last landed in a long-term rental house. The first night there I frantically went through all the suitcases, distraught that I could not find the boys' face wash. I couldn't handle one more whitehead, y'all. So I made a late-night run to CVS, snuck into my teenage boys' room with OXY wipes, and cleaned their oily, pimpled faces while they slept. For some reason, I felt it was my responsibility to make sure their personal hygiene and teenage acne was taken care of. Now, it was a little bit funny, except when one of them woke up, mumbling, "OMG, are you serious right now, Mom?!"

It's hard to let go of the desire to reach over and just change a loved one's choices, but that's not how relationships work. Attempting to control our friends, spouses, relatives—does this ever work out for the better? No. Does attempting to "declutter" another person help them feel loved? Decidedly not.

So we must unlearn both "hiding" our messes and avoiding looking at other peoples'. It's important to be honest about the fear of drawing close to others and letting them into the intimate messes of our lives and the stresses that will inevitably cause. It's so hard to approach people and risk vulnerability when you know that at some point, their issues are going to spill out into your life.

The subtle (or not) behaviors people engage in to avoid this comingling can take many shapes. We've seen friends marked as "serial daters" because they cut and run after the first few months of puppy love. Or we've caught ourselves and others becoming obsessed with a new friend, calling them all the time when the relationship is all sparkle and light, but when their pain or confusion over betrayal or disappointment starts to peep through, we find excuses for not having the same amount of time for them. Their struggles can rub us the wrong way or come up against our own limitations. Suddenly, a twinge of regret sneaks in.

To expect others to perform well and contain themselves past the first few times we are with them is not only unreasonable; it's an unhealthy way of creating deep friendship. I have pushed away friends because I needed something from them that I couldn't arrive at myself—I needed them not to be so freaking messy. *Sort yourself out* has often run through my mind when faced with someone else's mess. Why is that? Why do we hold people to a standard that we can't attain ourselves? It's suffocating, asking everyone to be so perfect. To come without their humanity. To come without issues. These expectations are socialized, and they start young.

We can start to build a narrative that we would be better off alone. We begin to keep our distance because the last time we got close to someone, we got hurt or lost control. We must keep reminding ourselves that people are not simple, and we can't predict what they are going to do. Predictability does not equal safety in a relationship. We can't control the outcomes of other people's choices.

Every time we add someone new into our lives, it's like adding another character into a story. The plot gets changed, and we don't know what the ending will be. We aren't the authors of others' life stories, only our own. So for control-happy individuals (like me), trying to dictate someone else's story is a minefield.

(Chris)

Own Your Own Junk

The other day, our friend Teresa was telling me about the social contracts she has had with various housemates. She had something like twenty-eight roommates over the span of a decade. It always irritated her that no matter how specific the house rules were, somebody (or everybody) had days where they just didn't keep up with their own dishes, backpacks, coats, or late-night-snack trash. It drove her crazy, until she started to notice all the exceptions to the rules she had for herself. An empty can of Diet Dr Pepper by the computer. A coat draped over the back of a chair. Leftovers hiding in the back of the fridge. It turns out it is impossible for any of us to leave what I call a "zero footprint."

Step 1 of "how to live with other people," then, is being in charge of your own self. Know your space. Take out your own trash and clean up your own room. Self-awareness—especially keeping a close watch on any self-talk that says you have to perform well in order to earn love—is vital to staying close to others.

Julie (and she has vetted this paragraph) is impatient. Her junk can look like being interrupted by an uninvited, unnecessary, non-urgent question by a clueless child and snapping at them as if they had tried to take her last piece of sea salt dark chocolate. She's also a little bit obsessive (her word). Julie may resolve to forgive someone who hurt her deeply, then scroll across an Instagram post and find herself launching into a sequence of four-letter words. All these little displays of humanity aren't a big deal in pieces, but the more she is in someone's life, the more they will affect that person, and she knows it.

My issues look different. I have learned to hide my messes because I don't like when other people see them. I like for people to think I have it all together. I hate wrinkled shirts and my kids' empty In-N-Out Burger sacks sitting in the back seat, but I have let the dirty dishes in my heart pile up. I am not the best at prioritizing everyday details. I might forget to pay a bill on time, or I delay putting new front license plates on our cars, so we get tickets when we park. (Pretty sure my tickets have personally funded the new overpass up the road.) I tend to avoid conflict, even when Julie needs me to fight for her. Performance and perfection are my drugs of choice. I'm still in recovery.

We both overperform, trying to present a picture of order and cleanliness to others, which is exhausting. I call it "dysfunctional self-presentation." It's a bad habit.

When someone steps in to see our mess for what it is, we discover we can relax a little. Take a seat and quit the act. We all have clutter.

The more honest we can be about the parts of us that cause friction for others, the freer we become to allow people in. It may be that you believe that you have really worked through your fear of being misunderstood, for example, but then your insecurity blows a fuse and gets in the way. It can come out of hiding without any notice and yell, "Oh look, even a best friend doesn't get you!" or "Wow, you don't even know yourself." Having grace for your internal messy room is a good idea. Your room doesn't stay clean forever; you have to keep picking things up along the way. Honesty is the way to love and receive love freely.

Julie and I are really aware when our struggles with scheduling and prioritizing spill into our kids' lives and our friends' lives, but we've noticed something rather stunning. Our kids still hug us. Our friends still call us. That means they are seeing and loving us as we are, without asking for perfection. We're inching closer to making a true home when we let each other in and don't pretend.

If you have been around religion, an influencer culture, or a red-carpet industry long enough, you become a master of the masquerade. But I think we are all tired of pretending, and it's showing.

Julie and I have a friend who grew up in a faith-filled environment and led a large ministry. Yet as a young man, he failed in such a catastrophic way that he had legal action taken against him. He was required to go to weekly therapy for ten years. Every Monday night he would sit around a circle with ten other men who had committed unthinkable crimes that deeply wounded others. He told us he had learned more about honesty, forgiveness, and wholeness by meeting with his small group of criminals than he had learned while a part of any other community. He learned how to be a mess without fear of judgment. We all need to get to a place where we are so finished with hiding, pretending, and performing that we bring our mess to the table.

(Julie)

Show Up Anyway

If making friends looked like a party invitation, it should read something like this:

COME TO MY MESS PARTY
Location and Time: TBD

That's not the easiest invitation to send, unless you have a healthy amount of self-compassion. I don't know about you, but drawing in others when I am feeling my messiest is hard. It requires a vulnerability that demands a brave surrender to our deepest fears, the most tender places we work hard to protect.

The last few years, my family has had front-row seats to how my close girlfriends in the GG have valiantly scaled my walls.

Because I was split open from my cancer journey, I was ready for growth and change. Yet it looked pretty awkward. It's not how I'd usually choose to make new friends: in the middle of a catastrophe and family trauma. Yet that's what I got.

Jess taught me how to be real with myself. She called me out every time I tried to perform at my own pantomime. She would say, "Stop doing that. Stop sabotaging your feelings. Feel it." It took me months to really internalize that message.

Sarah showed me my worth by showing up at my house over and over again with meals, gifts, parties, prayer, money—and on it goes still. Those actions opened my eyes to how I saw myself wrongly.

Teresa spoke hard truths when others might be afraid. She stopped me when my beliefs about myself were out of line, then showed me what she meant by loving me just like I needed.

Oh, and then there is Kristen, the PTF president at my kids' school, who pursued me when I could give her nothing. She still listens to all my word vomits and, yes, she cleaned up my *actual* vomit during chemotherapy. She tells me when I'm just managing my problems rather feeling them, and when I'm off kilter. She has been doing that since day one.

The disorderly mess that comes from pain or causes pain is meant to be shared. When it's protected and hidden, it only grows. And there are few things more painful than when our internal worlds look like a hoarder's house that no one is allowed into. Thus, we tell ourselves, *I'm fine. I can do this alone. It surely must be safer my way.*

The Three Commitments

So let us revisit our three commitments with some on-the-ground examples of what they look like. As a reminder, they are:

1. I admit that I can't control everything.
2. I will be messy around others.
3. I will let other people be complicated.

Here is what these commitments look like for me. I won't try to clean up my mess when someone catches me in the middle of a rant or a fear spiral or any of the other areas that I am actively working on. I will remind myself that I am allowed to have areas of growth and need in my life, and I will let them see it. This requires that I believe the best of my chosen family. It requires trust. But there have been times when I needed to have a verbal smack across the mouth to keep me from drowning in self-pity. Family loves us where we are and calls us up and out when needed.

I will not fake a perfect life, or—after listing the myriad things I'm crazy-busy with as a working person (or just dramatic person)—wrap it all up with a neat bow of contentment. That means I'll shut down my impulse to say, "When God shuts a door . . ." I don't need to. I pause and let other people see that my mess is a lot. I can tell the truth about my feelings, even if they don't make sense yet. I can accept other people's confusion; I won't try to tell them what to think. I'm going to choose to see mess as a sign that I'm successfully pursuing intimacy with other people, and I will congratulate myself for not bolting under pressure. Lastly, I will give myself permission to "not have it all together," and in return give others that same freedom.

I heard Craig Groeschel say recently, "You can have control or you can have growth, but you can't have both." Although he was referring to organizational leadership, this applies to us as individuals as well. More people means less control. More people will affect your time, your thoughts, and your atmosphere—and that's a glorious thing because our souls are not meant to journey in isolation. Our family has six people in one home. That's never been simple; each of us has had to learn to juggle and reassess. Organization without control. Managing in the midst of chaos.

Let me tell you about my dear friends Morgan, Charissa, and Caitlin. Last year, right after one of my major surgeries, I was trying to clean the garage, even though I was supposed to be resting. Neither I nor my family was getting anything done, but I was obsessing over the cluttered piles of mystery items.

After a firm rebuke over the phone, the three fairy godmothers came to my rescue. They sat me in a chair. (OK, they forced me into a chair.) They *dominated* that nauseating mess of a garage. While they worked their magic, I relished the moment: Caitlin's blaring music, tons of laughter, and futile efforts to keep me in the chair. I gained so much more than a clean and orderly garage complete with neatly stacked and labeled containers. My friends happily stepped into my mess and brought order not only to my garage but to the clutter in my brain.

Being patient with the complexity of others in relationship has never been my strong suit, in part because I felt so complicated myself for so long that I couldn't handle both. Once, a coworker rearranged my whole office without asking because she thought it would help me focus more. That same week she booked a meditation session for the two of us to work on "how we could become better friends and be more in tune with one another." I wanted to run far away! Instead, I put my office back to its original form and replaced the meditation session with a coffee date to understand what the deeper issue was. Seeking to understand before high-tailing it the other way or shutting down lets others be complicated.

Until recently, we lived within walking distance of the football stadium where Nate plays his home games. Last season we decided to have tailgate parties in our front yard a couple of hours before each home game. Usually, I would feel like we needed to provide the food and have it all beautifully arranged and displayed for our guests. But this year, we decided to have everyone bring their own food, and we would provide the drinks and lawn chairs. People still showed up for a quick meal and a good time. Then we would pack up and make the short walk together to the game, paper plates and cups strewn about the backyard for collection later.

I've missed too many moments trying to create a moment. Chris and I would look at each other often on those walks, laughing and catching each other's glance. *Isn't this it?!* we could hear the other saying. It sure is. Sometimes the mess is what makes the memory.

Commit

Our callout to you is pretty simple. Consider the three commitments we made, and reflect honestly: Which one sounds the hardest to address? Which is the easiest? Pick the one that seems easiest, and focus on fulfilling it. Let go of controlling others just a little bit more. Or let someone see more of your own disorganized life. Let someone in on your anxiety, and notice when they don't run for the hills. It's incomparable, even addictive, being loved despite your flaws.

Chapter 5

The Humility Factor

The mark of a true hero is humility.
—MASTER SHIFU, *KUNG FU PANDA*

(Julie)

I'm All Good

A few years into our marriage, Chris and I took a leadership assessment—one of those that first asks you to rate yourself from one to ten based upon certain categories like punctuality, ability to adapt, respect from others, and decision-making ability. We took our tests separately and then compared our answers.

"Punctuality. I gave myself a seven," Chris said.

"Oh. I gave myself a ten," I responded.

"OK. For leadership skills, I said six," Chris continued.

"I think I'm a ten," I said.

Then we got to the category of humility. Chris gave himself a six . . . and I gave myself (yep, you guessed it) a ten.

Chris laughed. "Jules, how do you give yourself a *ten* in *humility*?!"

My first reaction was defensive. "What? Why are you laughing?"

Then I got the joke. We both lost it. Tears sprang out of my eyes from belly laughing, and the rest of the day one or the other of us kept bursting into laughter. Clearly, I've never had an issue with self-esteem!

For most of my adulthood, I have had mile-high walls up when it comes to actually listening to outside voices that want to help me. This was apparent when I was first diagnosed with cancer. Eventually, I had to accept help—and advice. But I'm not the queen of humility, so this was a tough learning curve.

Take our family's nutrition, for example. Up until recently, we had been raising our kids on Little Caesars pizza (because Hot-n-Ready is a lifesaver), late-night cheese nachos in bed (because that's where the best convos happen), root beer (because that's healthier than Coke, right?), and a salad once a week (if we were lucky). We have always sat around the table for dinner, but "dinner" meant Taco Bell instead of a home-cooked meal. Since my first cancer diagnosis, I've had my fair share of holistic doctors and friends teach me how to turn that ship around. It's not easy to do when your kids have already established grown-up eating habits. Judging myself has felt easier than making change, and many time I have chosen to stay stagnant and prideful, and to engage in self-sabotage (eating doughnuts). Bottom line, it was hard for me to accept my ignorance about good nutrition. I had a choice: lean into humility or lean into stubbornness.

We know self-help is having a moment, and maybe you don't like it. Maybe you are one of those scoffing at the entire section of a bookstore dedicated to the self, but I tell you what . . . there's something there. I mean, the trend hasn't exactly hurt us. Less caffeine? We sleep better. More stretching? Our bodies move better. More awareness of our body types and "root issues"? Good information. But nothing transforms us more than listening.

What Chris and I have learned, especially since we married so young, is that you go through a lot more change when you stick around in relationships. So we should expect it, not as a by-product of relationships but as one of the reasons to stay in them. We need other people to help us grow. And no one grows faster than a person *willing to listen.*

Let me tell you two things that sum up a heart posture we need if we want to go "long haul" (or for the short-tempered, "any haul") with someone. Try saying these out loud (or whisper them to yourself when someone starts to irritate you), and see whether these convictions hit you the same way they hit us:

1. I don't know everything.
2. I can learn from you.

Turn over these statements on your tongue. If you let them sink in, they are like relational insurance policies: they hold you up when the flood comes.

(Chris)

"I Don't Know Everything"

In English, the word *humble* derives from the word for "earth"—*humus*.[1] Humility comes from the earth. It's both grounded and grounding. *Humus* is the organic part of the soil, produced by the decomposition of plant or animal matter, essential to the fertility of the earth.[2] Essentially, it is derived from death. The deaths of vegetable and animal matter create an environment for growth. In a real sense, we must practice a sort of "death of self" for our own growth and for the enrichment of others.

There's nothing more real than our humanness. Our hair falls out, our eyes need glasses, our hearing begins to grow faint—and if we aren't in touch with the fact of our fallibility, it's really hard to make close relationships go the distance because we think that every conflict is the another person's fault instead our own! Humility is a disarming force. It stops us at the moment we prepare to take up arms in a conversation and tells us, *Move inward. You're being unreasonable.*

Our friend Jeremie is a leadership coach, and he talks about the importance of having people in your life whom you trust and who can help you see how you come across to others—the tone of your voice, your body language, the stuff in your teeth. Sometimes we aren't ready to absorb those critical, teachable moments. Yet I believe they get planted inside us like seeds, ready to emerge when we are ready. The heart has to be soft, like soil that allows good and necessary things to grow. Wisdom for our souls never has to be wasted. Humility helps us to discover that we don't know everything.

One time I took a memorable thirty-six-hour drive from Waco, Texas, to Manhattan, New York, that began just hours after the Twin Towers tumbled to the ground. I ended up in a Ford Excursion with my best friend, Beau; a fellow pastor; a local mortician who was a member of FEMA; and a journalist from Connecticut. (This sounds like the setup for a joke, but it was real.) Beau and the journalist were sharing their favorite books and authors as I pretended to know who Socrates was and prayed they wouldn't elicit my historical knowledge. My recreation degree from Baylor didn't prepare me for this.

And then the moment I was dreading happened. Journalist Jeff turned to me and asked, "So what do you like to read?"

I cleared my throat and said six words that I immediately wanted to edit: "I'm not much of a reader."

Journalist Jeff looked around the crowded Excursion to see whether anyone else thought I was joking. But I wasn't. I looked down to avoid the glare. *Gulp.*

He began to do his best investigative journalism. "So what magazines do you read?"

"I don't."

"Newspapers?" Jeff persisted.

"Nope." I could feel myself dissolving into my tan leather seat. I looked at Beau with desperate eyes, screaming for him to make it stop.

Journalist Jeff completed his interrogation with one final, exasperated question: "How do you get knowledge?"

I took one more defeated gulp and responded with the only answer that I knew to be true. "I talk to people, and that's how I learn."

Beau smiled. Journalist Jeff looked away—unsatisfied, annoyed, and perplexed. And then there was silence.

I have looked back on that moment many times over the years. I'm more of a reader these days, but I would give that same answer if asked again today.

Ultimately, humility is about being a lifelong student and learner. It's about staying curious, refusing to let our quest for knowledge level off, and having a hunger and awareness that we can learn from anyone and anything.

(Julie)

Breakdown Mountain

Fighting for family means being open to the pain it can sometimes bring into our lives—and the humility of realizing when we are wrong. One Thanksgiving I got into a yelling match with my brother. One irritating moment after another had been burrowing under my thinner-than-I'd-like skin, and I ended up saying some four-letter words I will forever regret. Then I told my brother to get his family out of my house. Yikes. I can't remember what the trigger was except it was so small that even I was shocked when the words started pouring out of my mouth.

My brother and I have a history, as one has when you grow up with people. As siblings, we are as close as they come. But that Thanksgiving wasn't one of my prouder moments, to say the least. That choice I made hurt. I snapped because my ability to regulate my emotions was gone. My pain erupted and I could feel the volcano of heat spilling rapidly, sadly leaving behind a trail of relational casualties. Choosing family is becoming open to the process that pain beings into our lives—the pain of realizing when we are wrong.

I didn't discover the root cause of my irritability until months later, but the undercurrent was pain—which had nothing to do with my brother or his family. Pain hides in cracks and corners, and we like to forget it's there. So there are times when it comes out in the wrong moment and at the wrong person.

Once our pain has made itself known, we have two paths from which to choose: the path back down the mountain (hiding and/ or blaming others), or the path to a vista of humility and greater self-understanding. If we take conflict as an opportunity to learn about ourselves, we are able to see other people more clearly and with less judgment. The health of the relationship can be restored. My relationship with my brother was fully mended because I chose humility. He chose humility. I repented, and he forgave me.

I've learned that a superpower in relationships—whether with children, spouses, friends, or coworkers—is simply giving yourself permission to be flexible. Teachable. Weak, even. We tend to dislike the word *weak*, because—let's be honest—being weak doesn't get a great rep. But there should be nothing taboo about it. Weakness says, "I'm human. I'm grappling, stretching, reaching, hoping, and hurting." Admitting my inadequacies to a trusted group of people has been one of the best things I have done. I used to pride myself on being strong, but cancer became a relentless life coach, leaving me with no ability to simply power through.

So has letting others be strong for me when I couldn't. I've learned that I was both stronger and weaker than I'd thought. Every Bennett would nod at that.

Weakness is a form of humility that says, "I need help. I can't do it on my own." When we allow ourselves to be humble, we get something better in return: trust. Without trust, we get lost relationships. Without humility, we cannot disagree and remain close.

(Chris)

"Going Our Separate Ways"

The line "We're going our separate ways" is the opposite of what Julie and I live our lives for. Our hearts have broken hearing it from people around us. In the last few years we have received text after text saying, "My family has decided not to speak to me." Something is going horribly wrong regarding our general inability to navigate conflict with others in ways that result in restored relationships. It's so disheartening when we receive emails from long-beloved friends letting us know that they are suffering from depression or can't stop drinking because they feel so alone.

Is there a phrase being used in conversation more than "cancel culture"? We don't think so. We have seen the groundswell of cancel culture through mainstream media (both of the right-wing and left-wing varieties) polarize political parties and people. It seems that this mentality of "us versus them" has worked its way into how we relate to others. And while we are used to canceling things in our lives that no longer benefit us—like a landline phone, a streaming service, or a neglected gym membership—it should not be that simple to cancel a relationship.

This is important, and I hope it goes without saying (but you can never be too sure): *there are times when it is necessary to end a relationship with a toxic or harmful person.* Creating healthy boundaries is a necessity in dysfunctional relational dynamics. We are not suggesting that you need to stay involved in harmful relationships. There should be no tolerance for violence of any kind, and often leaving the situation involves help from the police or another specific agency to protect and provide the help needed. You need to (safely, and with the help of trusted people or professionals if needed) pull out of deeply unhealthy or abusive relationships in order for healing to begin.

But most of what I see around me is the flippant and reactive way that our culture views commitment. What happened to, "We're in this until the end, no matter what"? I find myself wondering, *Do these relationships still exist?* Are we willing to stand with our friends and family when they hurt us, misunderstand us, confuse us, disappoint us? When unconditional love is the tie that binds us, arguments and disagreements are talking points, not breaking points. I understand a relationship might need some space or time. But the haphazard cancellation of a person who once played a vital role in your life—that, I don't understand. People seem to be so easily able to erase history in an attempt to find "better" someplace else, and that needs to be examined.

Years ago I read *Humility* by Andrew Murray, a nearly pocket-size book that carries a novel-size message. He defined *pride* as "the loss" of humility.[3] In other words, to Murray, *pride* doesn't mean "I'm better than you" but instead, "I can do it without you." That book changed my life. Julie and I have decided we can't do life without each other. Or without others. We're needy like that—needy for learning with others.

We have a friend named Jim who is a kind, intentional, and open-minded family guy. He had always enjoyed a strong relationship with his parents. But over the last few years, differing views about politics, race relations, and vaccines created tension in their conversations. Then one day, about a year into this newer, uglier dynamic, Jim's parents told him they had decided to sever their relationship with him and their other kids who disagreed with them. In their minds, their preferences and convictions prevented them from intimacy. His parents turned to Facebook to find a community that agreed with them.

You may have a story similar to Jim's. Clubs, friend groups, businesses, and churches have grievously been split wide-open and divided. The COVID-19 pandemic heightened the already brittle social, political, and religious systems in society. Political parties have grown more divisive and vitriolic. Churches have closed their doors or never reopened after lockdowns. People have walked away from their old communities or found new ones that are built around "sameness." Some left because they needed to, when toxic leaders and subcultures were brought to the surface. Certainly, spaces that are filled with hate, bigotry, racism, misogyny, and the like need to change. There were some doors that needed to shut for good. But it seems to us that we have gone too far. We've shut the door to staying in relationship, when it's relationships that best transform minds and hearts—even or especially those that we disagree with.

In a military war, there is rarely complete agreement between opposing nations. But a willingness to come together for the peace and protection of the people is something that can be agreed upon. It's called an armistice, which is an agreement made by opposing sides in a war to stop fighting for a certain time; a truce. There are big issues in life that make us feel like ignoring them is somehow compromising who we are. But relational civil wars are being waged in so many areas of our lives based upon preferences. There is a difference between preferences and convictions. We don't have to agree with other people's convictions, but we can still respect them as people who are trying as hard as we are to do the right thing.

Convictions are built upon deep-seeded beliefs. They usually develop over time and through experience. I hold certain convictions that are directly related to my faith, and they will not change—and I don't believe they should. However, I don't expect others to carry the same convictions that I do.

Often, preferences are overemphasized and polarized when they should not be. Choosing to have creamer in your coffee versus drinking it black—the proper way, in my humble opinion—is a preference. Imagine me refusing to go to my favorite coffee shop, Common Grounds, with someone who only drinks their coffee au lait. Silly example, I know. But the bottom line is that I think we can find a lot more common ground (no pun intended) if we focused less on our differences and gather around our shared interests. It is possible to find ways to come together, to seek understanding, even if we don't walk in agreement. In other words, agreement is not a prerequisite to love. It's time to stop making every disagreement a war zone.

You know what Julie and I have been missing recently in the middle of all these long-distance potshots on social media, or even in school halls or radio interviews? Real, honest conversations that bring together diverse opinions and positions. Seeing leaders and friends listen to understand, even if we don't agree. I know that I am oversimplifying the American political climate, but I imagine few would disagree that there is a greater divide and polarization between people and political parties than ever before, and that isn't good. A survey Pew Research Center conducted in 2022 found that "72% of Republicans regard Democrats as more immoral, and 63% of Democrats say the same about Republicans."[4] Wow. No wonder we are reeling with division and isolation! What have we become? We are choosing preferences over relationships.

Shelving our pride to learn from another is life-changing. It's culture-making. Julie and I have had a lot of friends who think, believe, worship, and vote differently from us. Just a few years ago, I think we would have had a hard time finding commonality with them and would have made little, if any, effort to find it. Since our relocation to LA, we have discovered the beauty of diversity and have come to appreciate it. We have found ourselves asking questions that we never asked before. Some of the answers we've received have reinforced our beliefs, while some have caused us to go back and reevaluate. This has been really healthy and humbling for us. If we are students of life, then we can learn from other people even if we disagree.

One thing that could help is to sit down and write a list of your nonnegotiable values. How long is it? The more things on it, the less likely you are to "match" long term in any relationship. Is it a list of values or beliefs? If two people love each other (as friends or otherwise) but have different religious convictions, can they be close? We would argue yes—if they both have the common values of respect and humility. Julie and I have learned that many disagreements and disputes that lead to relational war are the result of either misunderstanding or prideful arrogance. It's easier to make a snap judgment, cut off the offending person, and walk away than it is to do the hard work of asking questions and seeking understanding.

So how do we position ourselves to learn from one another? We get to that second statement Julie mentioned earlier this chapter. It's a direct follow-up from the first one: "I don't know everything."

(Julie)

"I Can Learn from You"

The inability to or understand one another's differences makes it pretty hard to have cozy conversations, doesn't it? If someone is afraid that their dissent will cause an explosion or an expulsion, that fear starts to hover in the room. We have the power to change that by how we carry ourselves in each relationship. We can make a little bit of friction the norm.

Some of the most frustrating, irritating, and difficult people I've encountered are the same ones who have helped me grow the most. I know that learning through the irritation from others can form something precious in me, much like a pearl forms when an irritant breaks into an oyster.

But what about living out our "I can learn from you" statement in the parent-child relationship? We have chosen to parent from a place of equality rather than hierarchy. Chris and I don't know everything, and we don't see everything correctly all the time. When our kids were very young, we told them they had permission to tell us if we didn't respond kindly or if we mishandled a situation. As they got older and were more empowered to speak those things to us (respectfully), our eyes were opened. This has led to a lot of chats that forced us to grow in our parenting. Many times we've been called out on a harsh tone, unfair response, or a lack of listening. It would be easy to pull out the "because I said so" card, but it's not worth it to hold your pride as a parent and lose connection. When you build authentic trust with your children that is based on humility, the outcome is healthy, honest behavior devoid of shame and performance. This does involve irritation, but oh, the result is something raw and real and beautiful, just like the pearl.

We aren't going to sell humility to you as though being open to change is a barrel of laughs. It's not. But there's nothing healthier for you, and for your soul, than to be teachable. Is it fun when the kid you used to put in time-out for hitting his brother tells you that you are being rude? No. Do Chris or I enjoy a phone call with a strongly worded "Get your act together, Bennett. You're not living up to your potential" message from a friend? Obviously, no. We want every interaction to be a nonstop party of praise. But none of us really needs that—and *we wouldn't believe it anyway.* We need healthy doses of feedback. Without this vital change in our hearts toward humility, without choosing this value over and over, small conflicts turn into much larger fights, disagreements, and, potentially, breakups.

If we can't learn from each other, if we can't see frustration as a chance to grow, then we will get stuck. Shallow conversation will ensue. Ugh, so gross. Both Chris and I are basically allergic to conversations that go on and on with no real substance. In our family, we have practiced allowing friction so much that we have come to actually look forward to other people challenging us. It reminds us that we are in a process of transformation.

Well, That Was Embarrassing

Fallibility really is our best teacher. I lived most of my life not embracing it, unconsciously ignoring it, and most certainly betraying so much of myself in the name of trying to be better. I feel icky just thinking about how I tried to hide my flaws. What's interesting to me is that humiliating moments—where we really fail at being our best selves—can be such incredible pathways back to growth, as long as we turn away from shame and let humility lead.

It was early evening on a Saturday in Norman, Oklahoma, and our city was full of game-day traffic trying to inch out of the handful of streets that access the highway. "Boomer Sooner!" Except not too many chants could be heard on this day because the team had suffered a tough loss, and Oklahoma football fans don't take losses lightly. Norman goes into full-blown depression.

I blame the showing of my "humanity" that Saturday on the game's outcome. Ugh. If only they had won.

I was cooking dinner (at least attempting to) at home when I discovered I was one ingredient short. At the same moment, one of the kids had a diaper blowout, and I realized I didn't have a single diaper left. Now, I wish I could remember more details of what threw me so far over the edge, but clearly I have suppressed them. I just know that I desperately needed diapers, desperately needed to finish cooking, and was really angry at Chris for some reason. Chris stayed back, licking his wounds from my verbal tirade, while I proceeded to peel out of the circle driveway in my sexy baby-blue minivan with chrome rims, and plowed straight into our other car. My insides were on fire, and I was on a mission to Target, so instead of reversing, I just pressed the gas pedal harder. I stuck it to Chris by taking off half the paint on the side of his car. My ten-minute drive to Target took five minutes as I drove like a bat out of hell, still fully mad but now also fully shameful, which made my pride shoot through the roof of the car. Now, remember that game-day traffic I mentioned? Well, Target was extra crowded, and so was the parking lot.

There I was, my blinker claiming the parking spot that was about to open up, when a car aggressively swooped in from the other side. The woman driving gave me the head nod of delight and a chuckle as she turned in. I kept my middle finger up at her as long as possible, expressing my extreme disgust at her rudeness. But after soberly remembering I had already wrecked the van along with our other car in a matter of minutes (which would definitely make our insurance spike), I knew I should stand down.

So, naturally, I sped to the farthest spot in the lot, ready to get into fisticuffs in the Target parking lot.

As I sped up in order to reach the woman's car before she headed into the store, I said out loud, "Oh mercy, Lord, I need you to help me right now before I do something even more stupid. I'm too angry to chill myself!" And what do you know, about two steps before reaching her car door, I got whacked. Not by her; just . . . everything in me suddenly broke. I had wrecked the car. Driven too fast. Let my anger and frustration run me. Tears, sadness, and release came all at once.

The other woman stepped out of her car, also prepared to fight, and met my gaze.

Crying, I asked her for forgiveness. I said, "I've had a bad day, and I'm sorry for flipping you off over a parking spot." She broke down, too, and said she had had the worst day herself. Her dog had just died, and her husband was leaving her. Whoa. We actually hugged and laughed, and it was a *moment*.

Our mistakes can bring us personal breakthroughs. I've seen this with my kids, my husband, and my friends. It's hard to learn about ourselves—or others—if all we see each other do is succeed. It's the failures, the learning curves, and the work to grow into more mature selves (which never ends) that really connect us.

There are those times as a mom when I just start to yell—well, let's say raise my voice just a little louder—and then in the same tone I tell them how annoying such-and-such is (insert whatever it may be at any given moment). I'll lose my cool.

"Nate, how is it possible to loose another water bottle?"

"Joy, that is way too dramatic and emotional!"

"Brooks, you are out of control! Pull it together."

"Beau, stop being so sensitive. I can't handle it."

(And these are some of the nicer things I've spoken.)

Crash. As if giant cymbals are banging my insides together, I feel the reverberant waves of immediate guilt. Shame comes next, spilling over my whole body.

Humility allows me to see myself as vulnerable and imperfect. And I am reminded that *I am human, I am needy, I am fragile, and I shall apologize.* In times of conflict, I find that I'm often just reciting my narrative of frustration over my nearest and dearest because I'm actually irritated at myself or at my life. I must make the choice to reflect, to repent, and to be gracious, even if it means stopping midsentence to give myself a time-out.

(Chris)

A Clear View

I spent most of my teens and twenties with a distorted view of humility, but I didn't know it. I thought humility meant minimizing myself. Trying to make myself small in certain settings, like when I was around people older than me or people perceived as powerful. I wanted to believe I belonged, but inside I felt like an imposter. I would deflect compliments yet seek approval from others by performing my best. I wanted to be great but felt I needed to be meek. I lived in constant inner conflict.

I was at a small, three-day leaders' gathering a few years back where I was surrounded by people who were, in my eyes, spiritual giants. During a session, one of the speakers named Julian shared a definition of humility with me that reframed my view: "Humility is seeing yourself rightly." His words struck me in my heart. Humility is not degrading, disregarding, or displacing yourself; it's ultimately about knowing your worth and value and bringing this into every environment. Which is why Julie and I have cultivated the belief that our behaviors alone do not define us. Bad decisions and bad behaviors are part of our humanity, but they are not the summation of our identity. If we are seeing ourselves rightly, then we will have little problem taking responsibility for our actions without making excuses for them. Proper humility takes away shame.

We are all fragile. Cataclysmically fragile. Not robust, bouncy, easygoing—all the things I was told I would be once I was a grown-up. Nope. I'm still a small, touchy, but loving person who has issues. I've decided that our common, stubborn need to make things about who is right and who is wrong is probably driven by self-protection, holding everyone back from our unique inner lives and insecurities. Humility gives us the courage to let go of the need to self-protect.

(Julie)

The Great Surrender

This precious value of humility, this beautiful practice we are sharing here, is a life preserver because it remains even in the midst of hard times. Humility in family creates flexibility, softening our need for answers and perfection from one another. In recognizing that we are frail, we can go through any season together without losing the vision for why we love one another. And we can let go of control.

Our friend has a little garden (we don't have huge yards around these parts) where she is trying to grow blueberry bushes. She told me she became worried over the winter when the bushes lost their leaves, so she spoke with a gardener at one of the local nurseries. The gardener told her, "If you bend a branch slightly and it doesn't snap, it has sap inside. It may look dead, but it's going to bear fruit." This is so true of us, too, in and out of our flourishing seasons. We might not be in the best head or heart space—perhaps due to a health crisis, the loss of a loved one, or job loss—but even when our leaves have fallen and all the other signs of life appear to be gone, the flexibility of our branches is the telltale sign of life. That flexibility allows for growth and open-mindedness. We may feel as if we've brushed up against death, but in reality, we are just being bent, sat on, maybe squashed a bit. We need to do self-checks: Where are we a little dead inside? Where are we easy to snap and break when we encounter conflict in our families?

We must allow ourselves to bend and learn. To surrender to the truth that none of us are too far gone to drink some water and come back to life, to see ourselves rightly.

What if we all brought this level of humility—of teachability—into our relationships, constantly searching to understand before needing to be understood?

In the words of theologian Thomas Merton, "Pride makes us artificial, and humility makes us real."[5] We all need more "real."

Get Real

Here are some ideas for incorporating more humility in your life:

- On a sticky note, write down a phrase that stuck out from this chapter. If you don't know what to put, consider "I need other people" or "I don't need to be right." Then put the note on your bathroom mirror so you'll see it multiple times a day.
- Take a moment this week to write down your present needs. Be specific. Then consider asking someone to help you with one, such as grabbing a coffee together weekly or checking in on one another via text.
- Prepare a line to tell yourself the next time you get in a disagreement with a friend or family member. Say it out loud in the conversation. Something like: "I don't really understand your position. Can you help me see it differently?"

Chapter 6

Out of Bounds

"No" is a complete sentence.
—ANNE LAMOTT, *OPERATING INSTRUCTIONS*

(Chris)

Saying No with Gusto

During the COVID-19 pandemic, several friends of ours decided to add dogs to their households—and so did we. We call this a "COVID call":

> COVID call (noun): *A decision made during a pandemic that an individual never would have made otherwise, such as learning the art of sourdough or buying a bouncy canine.*

Our kids have begged for a dog for years. We came up with some terms of agreement: said puppy must be adorable, be small- to medium-size, and involve absolutely no shedding.

Enter Champ—our fluffy, apricot, fun-loving stuffed-animal-look-alike goldendoodle. I am obsessed. I'm pretty sure over the last year I've taken more pictures of Champ than of our own children. He has been an incredible gift to our entire family and brought us lots of joy amid lots of hard stuff. We hired a trainer to help him master potty training and learn how to fetch our coffee. (Well, I wish the latter were true.) Thankfully, we have a great fenced-in backyard that allows him lots of room to run around and play. Currently, Champ is 90 percent obedient, but that remaining 10 percent has nearly cost him his life a couple of times. We still must watch him like lifeguards on duty anytime the front door opens because he will rocket outside before we can yell his name. We have reverted to bribing him by saying, "Treat, treat, treat," until he hauls back inside to take us up on the offer. (OK, maybe we need the trainer to come back.)

There have been a couple of times that our tasty incentive wasn't enough, and Champ took off like the running bulls of Pamplona. One time, he ran right at a car cruising down our street, which barely missed him. The safety of a fenced-in back-yard brings some limitations, but ultimately it provides safety and peace of mind (other than the possibility of stepping in the sporadic poop around the lawn).

When we remove or ignore our boundaries, we become vulnerable to more than we can handle. Certainly Champ had no intention of running into oncoming traffic, but he wasn't aware of the car, nor could he have changed the car's course. We need clear boundaries in our lives and relationships so we don't get run over.

So what do we mean by *boundaries*? Boundaries are healthy limitations and values. We like this definition: "The limits and rules we set for ourselves within relationships. A person with healthy boundaries can say 'no' to others when they want to, but they are also comfortable opening themselves up to intimacy and close relationships."[1] They allow us to grow and thrive without overextending ourselves. We all have our limits, and boundaries help us identify them—for ourselves and for those seeking relationship with us. However, as we will discuss in this chapter, boundaries aren't a complete safeguard against conflict in relationships. They do keep many problems at bay, but they can't protect us from them all. However, a life without boundaries is like keeping sheep without a fence: you basically lose all your stock. At least with a fence, you have a fighting chance.

Julie has never been a big fan of rules. They make her armpits sweat. I, on the other hand, love rules. They make me feel safe. Yet we both have been slowly learning that the real soak-through-your-shirt kind of sweating comes when there are *no* fences. Healthy boundaries help to create healthy relationships, and the converse is also true. Communicating my needs and capacity in certain seasons has brought a real sense of freedom that's hard for me to explain.

This type of communication takes courage. Not everyone will understand or appreciate it; some will even be offended by it. But we can't be responsible for how others respond to our boundary setting.

Looking back, I spent years overextending myself with the countless needs of people who came in and out of our lives. Because I was a pastor, I felt that this just came with the job. I had to put others first, no matter the cost. Evenings would be filled with meeting obligations to other people and events, and though our kids were along for the ride, I know it sometimes felt like they didn't have a choice.

About five years into our ministry in Oklahoma, our family took a three-week sabbatical. We went to Colorado to unplug and relax. The first few days there, I sat alongside a rushing river that careened through the town of Breckenridge. My body felt like that rushing river: my heart was racing, and my mind couldn't be still. I was exhausted. I was heavy and discouraged, and I didn't know why. It was as if the Check Engine light of my soul had been blinking for months, and I had chosen to ignore it in hopes that it would go away. This is how I have dealt with lots of issues over the years: avoidance. Disguise everything in a shiny thought or a forced smile and ignore the pain.

Over the next couple of weeks, I began to journal my thoughts without editing them like I usually would. I released my raw, honest feelings. I wasn't sure I wanted to keep being a pastor. I didn't know if I had it in me. The church was growing, but I was withering.

When we came back from our time away, I began to make changes. I stopped saying yes to every invitation and slowed down my travel. I was committed to getting myself back to a place where I was thriving, and putting healthy, clear boundaries in place was my first step toward healing.

It's easy to fall into the trap of wanting to be a "super friend" who overflows with boundless love. But we can't bring that level of intimacy to every relationship. I had to learn that having my own clear expectations allowed me to respect the limits of other people, of organizations, and even of Julie. Changing what I believed every interaction should be freed my heart to lean into and respect each different connection I have.

Our time is a precious commodity, and not everyone can have access to it. Prioritizing our relationships helps us ration our time. Julie always says that some people are "drop by for a minute" friends. Some are "long talks at midnight" people. Some are "holiday party" people. Our capacity to give fluctuates in different seasons of life. So you have to know your situation, determine your capacity, and then set your priorities so that you know whom to engage with and who will have to wait.

A Short List of Priorities

Your boundaries protect your priorities. As a husband, father, and pastor, I have learned (painfully) that you can only have so many key goals. If the list is longer than five, you'll end up forgetting some of them.

We have a friend who has to be at work early, and it's really important for her to be rested and vibrant for her workplace so she can give emotionally after work to her roommates. Her rule is that she goes to bed early if she is working the next day, and she follows through, regardless of what fun event might be occurring. It's admirable, she's consistent, and she is a better friend for it.

Here are some of the Bennett family's top priorities:

- Be present with others.
- Take risks.
- Love others without judgment.
- Do things that are fun.
- Respect the boundaries of others.

So how do these factor into our boundaries? Here's one example: If one of the kids tells me they're not ready to talk about their day yet, that they need space to do something like play basketball or chill out, I let them have that. I don't barge in and insist that they share their whole day right off the bat. It's not my place to impose my timeline for communication on them. And each of our kids processes things differently, so Julie and I wait until they are ready. This applies just the same with roommates or other close relationships. Communication in your various community settings is key, and honoring boundaries is one way we show respect.

Boundaries with Children

Julie and I often have to fight to schedule time for just the two of us, something that is vital to a healthy marriage. Our kids have historically struggled to honor our time alone. They will walk into our bedroom unannounced (which could be a scarring experience for them, depending on the time of day), or interrupt and talk over us while we are in the middle of a conversation. When they do this, they are crossing a line, and we must keep reminding them that doing so doesn't build trust or honor our marriage. We may end up locking our door (to set a firmer boundary) or going out to talk. Julie and I do whatever it takes to have this time together.

We have found language like this to be helpful with our children: "Kids, we love you and value being present with you. Mom and I have had a difficult time connecting this week, and we need some focused time to get on the same page. We need you to give us the next hour to have uninterrupted time together, and when we are ready, we will let you know. Will you please respect that?"

Boundaries with Our Partners

It might seem weird to talk about establishing boundaries with our life partners, but it's important. I'm an internal processor. Julie is an external processor. Julie is also a fixer and wants resolution, whereas I tend to avoid and ignore. We have had to learn how to respect our differences and to make rules to ensure that happens. In the early years of our marriage, if we got into a fight, Julie would want to duke it out right then and there. That never went well, because I needed space to sort out what she had said. We would both end up saying things that we regretted. She has learned to respect that I often need time to process how I feel before I communicate. I have learned that I can't expect her to stuff down her feelings for long.

We have always tried to live with each other in an open and honest way, not forcing vulnerability but inviting it in. Boundaries help us not to avoid conflict but rather engage in it in a healthier way.

Here are some "fences" Julie and I have placed around our communication to work through conflict:

- We give time to be ready before connecting over something, big or small.
- We ask for specificity, so we are discussing tangible issues instead of obtuse feelings.
- We ask for space to speak without being interrupted.

We also keep boundaries in other areas of our relationship, such as making sure the other person has what they need outside of the partnership. We guard one another's free time to work out or to connect with friends as if it were our own time. We celebrate each other's trusted friends. Yes, we are married, but we recognize that having friendships and activities outside of our marriage makes us better partners.

Boundaries with Friends

Ready for something that sounds brutal but is really very practical? We have come to realize we cannot prioritize every relationship. We deeply love our friends, but the older we get, the tighter that circle of "anywhere and anytime" friends becomes. And even then, that "any" comes with quite a few caveats (called *our children*), meaning our kids will always come first. In college, we would give our time away to anyone who wanted it. We had not set up boundaries, so every time we went outside of what a healthy relational expenditure would be, we paid an emotional price.

Here are some tips as you consider your friendships:

- Recognize your capacity in the current season. How much time and emotional bandwidth do you have for friendship? However much or little time you have, guard it.
- Let friends know your timeline for returning texts and calls, and stick to that. You don't need to text or call anyone back right away.
- Prioritize your alone time. Consider how much time you need and then protect it, even if you have a busy week.
- Pick a night every week that is designated for time with friends. Protect that time.

(Julie)

Way Too Wide-Open Spaces

When you fly, there's a point during the preflight safety demonstration when the flight attendant says something to the tune of, "In the case of a loss in cabin pressure, oxygen masks will drop from the ceiling. Please make sure to secure your own mask first, and then turn and attend to the person next to you." This is important advice. You can't secure someone else's mask if you've passed out.

After my second cancer diagnosis, I sought holistic treatment in Spain with Dr. Hilu, a leading cellular biologist. He has a microscope that can magnify a person's blood sixty-five thousand times so he can see what is happening inside your cells and the effects it is having on your body. Being the blunt, cut-to-the-chase person that I am, I asked him to tell me what he saw in my blood. He looked at me and said this, which has stuck with me to this day: "You need to be selfish. You have to stop worrying about everyone else and make yourself the priority."

Growing up in the church, I was constantly told that selfishness is a sin. Deny yourself. Put others first. Those are concepts that can be misused and abused if we aren't careful. In the Gospels, Jesus would often go away alone, far from the needy, hurting, and demanding crowd that collected around him everywhere that he went.[2] Was he being selfish? What about all the people who needed to be healed? He knew what we all need to learn: our impact, love, and service can only flow from a place of fullness and rest. This is why boundaries are essential.

I've worked hard to help my children build boundaries early on. As adults, it's our job to ensure the most vulnerable are aware of what appropriate boundaries look like. Parents can have one-on-one conversations with their children in different seasons of their lives, asking appropriate questions, listening, and then educating them on how to protect themselves. This intentionality becomes a fence of safety around your little ones.

Helping your children understand the world and the dangers in it doesn't have to be as heavy as it can seem. No matter how uncomfortable you may feel, when you are honest in your communication and come from a place of connection, the words will come. But glossing over and dumbing down the hard topics because you're afraid of the conversation never helps. These conversations are a gift I wish I was given when I was younger. Conversations about what it looked like to love how I was made while protecting it as my own. Conversations that provided clarity about consent. But I am choosing to give that gift to my children, especially my daughter, Joy. I am modeling respect—of her process, her questions, and her emotions—in a safe and shame-free zone.

Having limits can sometimes seem unkind to people who don't understand our intentions, but they are one of the kindest things we can do for ourselves. Chris and I can tell when we have overstepped, ignored, or had our boundaries violated by the amount of peace we feel. Violated boundaries create restlessness and exhaustion. Our level of enjoyment of a relationship is in direct proportion to our willingness to put up boundaries. This sometimes means walking away from those who are clamoring for our attention. We had to ask someone we deeply loved to move out of our house because boundaries had been crossed— and it wasn't completely their fault. An emotional dependency had developed that was making constant withdrawals from our overdrawn accounts. Our guest didn't understand, but that is OK—not everyone will.

I've had to really work to put my finger on why setting boundaries sometimes feels strange to me. Some of it is my wiring, some of it is fear, and some of it is pride. There are beautiful parts of my personality that make me wild and fierce. But wild stallions don't do very well when first put inside a fence. Honestly, I get an anxious twinge just thinking about those poor horses before they get "broken" (an unfortunate term, really). But though I am a human (and not a horse), the wonderful, wild, and untamed parts of me still need the safety of knowing where the boundaries of my relationships are.

We need to be clear about what boundaries are and aren't, because if we are confused, they can be used against us. I have sat in a room with religious peers and leaders who told me that I had too many boundaries (when they wanted me to work more) or not enough boundaries (when they felt I was too involved with a decision). My boundaries have been used as a silencing tactic when a person who overstepped them shamed me for my own lack of self-protection. I sometimes haven't had the right kind of boundaries—like when I've required people to explain themselves when they impose unwarranted criticism on me. Or when I've allowed eye rolls and glares when I spoke "out of turn" in an all-male setting.

In the past, I've reacted to people imposing their restrictions on me by equating *restrictions* with *boundaries*. So for a while I threw the idea of boundaries off me, thinking, *Screw it. I can't win anyway!* But boundaries can be lifelines when chosen and not forced. They are not shackles but guidelines to show us how to handle one another with love and respect.

You might be familiar with what Jesus called the two "greatest" commandments: "Love the Lord your God with all your heart and with all your soul and with all your mind," and "Love your neighbor as yourself" (Matthew 22:37–40). Love others as you love *yourself*. Establishing boundaries is one way to do that. As selfish as it may feel, making your own health and care a top priority is a necessity to create healthy relationships. We can only love others to the extent that we love ourselves. It's just the way it works. When we determine our relational priorities, we are able to instinctively say yes to what we should do and respond with a guilt-free no to what we shouldn't. A lack of boundaries violates, while healthy ones honor us.

Honoring Each Other's Boundaries

It's hard to stick to your boundaries all the time. So it's OK, and often necessary, to exercise humility by asking others for help with this. It's really important that we convey our boundaries to the people closest to us, and then let one another be a little bit "in charge" of enforcing them.

Those who know me know I have a bad concept of time. My inner clock has caused more stress than I can express because my best ideas and bursts of energy often come at the last moment. The other night I went out to hang with my girlfriends, knowing I had to leave on a 7:00 a.m. flight the next morning. My conversation with Chris sounded something like this:

Julie: Hey, babe, I promise I'll leave by nine and be in bed by ten.
Chris: *(Eye roll. Another eye roll. Sigh.)* Are you kidding? You will be home by nine? Is that a.m. or p.m.?
Julie: Babe, seriously. I'm exhausted. I'll leave at nine.

Chris: *(texting at 9:30 p.m.)* Where are you? Thought
    you were leaving at nine.
Julie: *(texting)* Hey! I'm about to leave!

10:45 p.m.: Julie pulls up in the driveway.

Next day: Julie pays the price through exhaustion.

I could have stayed out much later, believe it or not. My girlfriend, unbeknownst to me, had texted Chris last week and said: "Hey, I'll make sure Julie is out the door and headed home by nine." If she hadn't hounded me that night, ten forty-five could have been midnight! Old Julie would have been ticked off at the friend. She would've said right there, "Don't manage me and tell me what to do!" New, beat-up, and healing Julie felt loved and grateful. It's a beautiful thing when you have family around you that not only honors your boundaries but helps you protect them.

Pre–cancer journey, my lack of boundaries regarding my time and, most often, my emotional energy and well-being invited needy people to trample my soul. And I took it, again and again. Those of us who have a tendency toward a "savior complex" can be unaware of this habit because it's deeply ingrained in our DNA to be there for others. I'm not saying we aren't supposed to have times when we turn our lives upside down to serve others, but it cannot be at the expense of our own health.

In the past, I have ignored internal warning signs to the detriment of my family. When my son Brooks was only a month old,

I stayed in the hospital all week with someone in need because I wouldn't leave her side. He slept with me in the recliner in her room. This was noble at first, but it passed the lines of health and sanity. I wouldn't let others take on the responsibility. I felt that it was on me. And I paid the price.

Early in our marriage, Chris and I would invite people with substance-use disorders to stay with us even though our kids were struggling with needing our full attention. We would give money away to pay other people's bills but couldn't pay our own. This over-attentiveness to the needs of others resulted in physical and mental exhaustion, and while others thought I was at peace, I was faking it. I want to reiterate that helping others and sacrificing is part of how we are supposed to live in community, but not when it keeps us from being whole. Healthy boundaries must be clear, communicated, and mutually understood or else unhealthy people will ignore the Private Property sign that got covered up by the overgrown weeds of our neglected hearts.

It's important to allow space for different categories of influence and intimacy. This is vital to help prevent unrealistic expectations so you can enjoy relationships for what they actually are. One of the most powerful boundaries we can create comes in the form of permission to choose. We get to choose who is the closest to our hearts, who gets access to the deepest places of our souls. For years I believed a lie that love says everyone gets all of me. I don't want you to make the same mistake.

There's no perfect system for forming boundaries. You create them on the road to self-knowledge. Some boundaries can be fluid, as you keep listening and changing with your closest people, for everyone's health and growth. We must to learn to set boundaries on who exactly our family is and then become wildly committed to forgiveness. There's no other way to make a home.

Go Back

Return to the sections earlier in the chapter that discussed creating boundaries in different types of relationships (with partners, children, and friends). What resonated with you? Can you imagine having a conversation with that friend who always complains you don't answer their texts quickly enough? If that idea upsets you, then it probably needs to happen. Write down what you need to protect the most in your life. Do you need to create space for time in nature amid your busy days? Do you need to guard that once-a-week class you take, or extend it into an evening with friends? Or do you need to set a boundary with your partner about how, when, and where you have "deep talks" or discuss conflict? Be honest about what you need and what you can manage to give to others, and implement those boundaries.

Chapter 7

The Big B

*For there to be betrayal, there would
have to have been trust first.*
—SUZANNE COLLINS, *THE HUNGER GAMES*

(Chris)

The Dangers of Letting Someone In

There have been many times that Julie and I have gone into
military cleanup mode in the rush of having a guest coming
to our house. One of us makes a list, and we hand out chores to
every person, oldest to youngest, to cover all our bases. We need
everything to be perfect. Spotless. We ensure that the visible
parts of our home, like the kitchen and living room, look pris-
tine. Pillows are tilted the correct direction, and a lit candle sits
on our fireplace mantel to create ambience. *What a beautiful*

space, you would think upon seeing it. But there are places that you can't see. Our cleanup only goes so far. The bedrooms are shut and double-locked. We might as well put caution tape over the bedroom doors. Guests aren't allowed to wander down our halls.

Think of the people closest to you. Would you be willing to let them show up unannounced and go into your bedrooms and closets? Would you worry they would judge you? Would you feel compelled to provide an explanation for your mess? As people become your family, you begin to give them special access to areas of your life that are off-limits to most. Access brings great risk. Healthy boundaries can limit the inadvertent damage to a relationship, but it can't always prevent or predict betrayal.

In World War I, American fighter pilots covering a plane's rear position coined the phrase "I've got your six." This mantra morphed into the more common phrase "I got your back." And while we have known friends, coworkers, and relatives who have "had our backs," on the flip side, many of us have also experienced being "stabbed in the back" by the people we thought had it covered.

A skilled sniper can take out an enemy from over one thousand yards. It takes incredible skill, training, and nerve to be able to pull off a strike from this distance. But these are not the kinds of wounds we receive from family. A fatal blow from family often takes place by nature of proximity and relational influence. Healthy relationships are formed on the premise of safety; they're meant to be a place where we can let our guard down. Where we can check our weapons at the door and come to the table defenseless in our words, actions, and intentions.

The Bennett family has experienced every kind of betrayal story—in our marriage (which we will discuss in the next chapter) and with our children, friends, and individuals in our work community. I once had a mentor, someone I had openly shared the struggles of life and leadership with. Then one day he turned on me. My leadership was undermined and my vulnerabilities were used to question my ability to lead. In the moment, when family (or someone who feels like family) turns on you, the situation feels irrevocable, and you feel inconsolable.

Betrayal is the act of violating a person's trust, hopes, or expectations. A friend of mine once defined it as "an adultery of the heart." The word *betrayal* isn't applied to any instance where you are annoyed or irritated. You don't say that your mailman or your grocer betrayed you. No, it's the people closest to you who can wound like this—the best friends, the close coworkers, the favorite relative. Being stabbed in the back is most likely to happen from those we thought had our backs. These types of wounds are often the most painful because we didn't expect them. We didn't expect our trust to be used against us.

The concept of betrayal is ancient—biblical, even. The first time "sin" is mentioned in the Torah is when Cain murdered his own brother, Abel. In Greek mythology, at the order of his mother, Rhea, Zeus overthrew his father in order to become ruler. It was one of Jesus' twelve *handpicked* followers who would end up selling him out and turning him over for a bag of coins (which is why, incidentally, the number thirteen is considered to be unlucky. It's the number of those at that fateful dinner that included Judas, the betrayer). In 1836 the Native Americans felt the sting of betrayal when the United States government forcibly removed them from their land. Julie is a part of the Cherokee Indian tribe and shared with me how even after a large majority of Cherokees signed a petition, known as the Treaty of New Echota, to prevent the loss of their territory, around five hundred Cherokee Indians (claiming to represent the sixteen-thousand-member tribe) still made the deal, leaving many feeling betrayed. Treachery is a blight on humankind and a tragic theme across cultural stories. If we choose to open ourselves up for the sake of intimacy, then betrayal can happen to us too.

We've covered that there are a lot of ways we can set ourselves up for healthy intimacy. Yet even when we have right expectations, those closest to you can hurt you the most. Family is granted access to a space inside you that is sacred. These are the people to whom you have given a backstage pass to your life.

Julie and I are making an argument for both the safety that boundaries bring but also the risk that comes with inviting others inside your heart.

(Julie)

Goes with the Territory

One morning while writing this chapter, we received a text from someone who has felt betrayed by us. Someone who had trusted us and worked alongside us. Our painful decision years earlier to remove this person from their position in our church has had a lasting impact on their entire family. They are still grieving and trying to heal. We have reached out many times over the years to repent of our handling of the situation. We could give a dozen reasons to justify our behavior and make ourselves feel better, but the truth is, we caused real and lasting pain.

Apologies cannot come with defenses and long-winded explanations so we don't feel so crummy. Chris and I did not act like family, bottom line. In our text exchange, we acknowledged the pain we had caused and again asked for forgiveness. The other person responded by admitting that they continue to feel hurt, but they are willing to work toward forgiveness.

Making amends does not mean there has to be restoration of the relationship. There are no shortcuts for grieving these types of wounds. As Brené Brown said in an interview: "Grief does not have a timeline. It takes as long as it takes."[1]

If we are not careful, due to our own past wounds, we can retaliate against those who thought they were our allies. All it takes is a little stab with our words to cause a lot of bleeding. As the proverb goes: "The words of the reckless pierce like swords" (Proverbs 12:18).

Betrayal is the wound that Chris and I have found most of us spend a lot of energy trying to avoid or to recover from. It comes in many forms: a misunderstanding that becomes willful when one person refuses to see the good in another; a purposeful, selfish sabotage; or a sudden drop-off in communication. So what do we do when it happens?

When They Walk Away

For years Beth and I were the best of friends—"To the end" kind of friends. But then change and transition entered our lives, and we didn't communicate about how this affected our relationship. After some time passed, the floodgates opened, and there were some *big* feelings released. The things she shared were painful. I thought this was an easy fix, that we simply had different perspectives. It turns out she felt we each had unmet expectations of the other person, which of course was fueled by our different perspectives. I felt like Beth wasn't willing to fight for our friendship, which I thought was solid. But that was only how I saw it. She needed time. For lots of reasons, it was clear we weren't safe for each other anymore. But it felt deeply unfair because our relationship was something we both valued. She let go without asking whether I was ready.

I felt like I had failed some ultimate friend test. As I started sorting through the rubble of our relationship, here is what I found: I was expecting her to act like I would have. As I recently heard someone say: "Stop expecting *you* from other people." I do that sometimes. And my pain over our distance was not just about her.

The cleanup of this rift has been an ongoing journey into recognizing my deep fear of not belonging and not being fought for by the people I perceive to be the closest to me. And my definition of what "fighting for me" would look like is narrow. Even if we drift apart from someone, we can still learn from them. In some ways, the breakdown with Beth was a gift because it parked me in the repair shop for quite some time. In reflection, I still feel twinges of pain, but I can now reflect on how the unexpected conflict served to unearth my own fears and thus helped me to lean into making my own family more whole.

So what do we do when it doesn't feel like the other side is willing to meet us in the middle? When they don't see the same need to seek understanding, to keep talking? When they refuse healthy communication to be able to move on? I have learned that all we can do is to keep our side of the street clean. That is, each of us is responsible for only our own actions and emotions. If we only focus on feeling misunderstood or disrespected, we will miss the opportunity to be repaired in the ways we deserve.

Types of Betrayal

Treachery feels like a word for a spy who has deceived his country and given up information that could affect millions of people. That sounds a little dramatic, but it is a *big* word. Ultimately, though, we engage in treachery *any time that we disregard or violate something entrusted to us that is precious to those we love.* There are so many ways to do this, and it's helpful to spell them out so we can reflect on whether any remind us of situations we're in or actions we might be taking without knowing it.

A Betrayal of Trust/Confidence

A betrayal of a family member's or friend's trust is sometimes minor and can often be stitched up with an apology, unless it becomes a pattern. It could be that you shared something personal with someone who didn't keep that information private. Immediately, the confidence you had in that person is betrayed. Or perhaps you are the one who passed along something you shouldn't have. You might find yourself in this situation when you believe that someone else's information is yours to share, and that you have a right to discuss it how you want. You fail to consider how your friend or loved one would feel about it.

A Betrayal of Belief

Sometimes we assume that someone sees the best in us but find out through time or circumstance that this wasn't the case. You discover that a person misjudged your intentions and was not honest about how they saw you. You hear gossip through the grapevine or notice a shift in that person's behavior toward you, but they have not had a direct conversation with you about their feelings. This is so painful because you had been living with the assumption that the other person was for you. Your trust in them is now broken.

A Betrayal of Loyalty

People talk about being loyal to a certain restaurant or a sports team, but that is not what we are talking about here. The loyalty we look for in family is messy, hard, honest, gritty, and devoted. If you are familiar with the TV show *The Office*, then imagine Dwight Schrute and his fealty to his boss, Michael Scott. Loyal people don't scare easily; they aren't looking for a way out. They don't have to always agree with you to be willing to stick around. You need to know that you have people who will call you out on your crap, hold you accountable, and love you just the same. Loyalty means "I won't abandon you when you are struggling, and I will choose to give you the benefit of the doubt for as long as I can." Loyalty is not something that is given out flippantly or too quickly; it is earned. To betray loyalty in a relationship takes a pattern of someone talking negatively about you to others, not seeing through your moments of weakness to the best of who you are. It feels like a loss of support and happens only with those people with whom you have a deep or intimate relationship.

A Betrayal of Boundaries

Betraying boundaries is when you have established healthy limits to your time and relational capacity with friends, coworkers, or family, and those boundaries are constantly disregarded and overstepped. When this happens more than once, it becomes a real betrayal and makes you want to withdraw or sever the relationship. You often find yourself wanting to avoid people who betray your boundaries because you feel they don't respect you.

The Full Monty: A Betrayal with Intent

When you are very close with someone, a part of you says, "I believe you'll put me first." This is the mutual trust of spouses. Best friends. Even parent to child. I believe that Chris would take a bullet for me. I know I would for him. For our kids. For those I love deeply. But sometimes—many times—we don't. We put ourselves first. And while that's to be expected, there is a time when the "me first" has the potential to destroy a relationship. Especially when it is manifested by only the most vicious of behaviors: stealing from your children, adultery, malicious slander of a friend. We've done these or experienced these, and they are a hard hurdle to clear.

As much as we say that what we have done is "not about you," it absolutely feels like it's about you when you are the injured party, and it's nearly impossible to feel loved after this type of betrayal. These types of injuries can prompt you to live carefully, guarding your heart and attempting to predict who will betray you and who will not. But the more you do this, the more you harden your heart. You stop trusting anyone and start withholding your love, making it impossible to experience true intimacy.

Removing the walls around the heart takes time. I'm forty-four, and my first big betrayal happened after being sexually abused as a little girl. I was betrayed by someone my family knew. I still have to revisit that eleven-year-old little girl at times in an attempt to remind her that she's safe now. I say *now* because it happened again when I was fourteen, so I also go back to *her* sometimes and hold her close. Betrayal of trust, of body, of hope—those painful experiences are the primary reasons why I learned to identify and put up healthy boundaries that have come from learning to truly know my worth. I no longer let my voice be silenced by fear and manipulation to feed another's gain. When it's in my power, I will not put myself in settings where I may be taken advantage of. I can say no. I can tell the truth and be safe. Yet looking at little Julie, I know that it is not her fault that she didn't have strong enough walls against what happened. She was double-crossed and tricked. She thought she was safe with someone, but they had lied to her. It's a deep wound—one that takes a long time to heal and leaves a scar. I am so grateful to Chris for his kindness and tenderness as he has walked with me through every phrase of my healing.

So many people have felt this betrayal, and it's more than we can handle in this book. But I wanted to include my story because the words are important to say: if you were abused, then you were betrayed. It wasn't your fault, and I'm so sorry. Because walking through the healing process can be complex and scary, I recommend finding a safe person, such as a licensed therapist or mental health professional, to help along the way.

Betrayal can also take the form of surprise attacks on our jobs or by those we work with. I will never forget the evening when Chris and I were gathered in our living room with a handful of leaders whom we had let into our lives and given permission to speak into our leadership. This meeting happened once a year and was intended to be a safe place for us to process our challenges and struggles in order to receive wisdom and feedback so we could keep growing as leaders. The conversation turned on us, and it was us (vulnerable) versus them (armed). We wish we had said, "That's enough; this isn't appropriate," but we didn't. There are few things as painful as feeling like you're being thrown in front of a firing squad who doesn't see the best in you. We were pulling shrapnel out of our backs while trying to heal from each new shot. We are aware that not every story like this has a happy ending, but amazingly, after hours and hours of hard, honest conversations, we were able to come to a place of healing and reconciliation with these spiritual leaders.

These things still happen to us in our forties, and they may even happen in the decades to come. That's just how it is when you choose to let people into your life. We turn on one another, whether with malicious intent or due to our own self-protective

or foolish tendencies, in ways that can really harm our connections. This is when we need the ability to not only say hard
things—to confess our pain and frustration to one another—but
also to forgive.

Processing the Past

We hope that in reading some examples in this chapter of different ways we can betray or be betrayed in close relationships, you were able to identify both tendencies you might have (like not believing the best of others) or things that particularly hurt you (like people telling others information you shared in confidence). Take some time to sit by yourself and take three slow, deep breaths. Check your body and mind to see if any pain has stirred up that needs to be addressed. Are you a loyal friend? Do you seek to be more true, kind, and trustworthy? Is there someone you need to tell the truth to about how they have hurt you? Be brave and honest, but also give yourself time. These are big feelings to process. Hopefully, you can see whether there are patterns in your life or relationships that need some painful and honest reflection. There's hope, if you find those tendencies (maybe with the help of a counselor), that change can come.

Chapter 8

Drop Off the Baggage

There is no future without forgiveness.
—DESMOND TUTU

(Chris)

Believing the Best

I will never forget the day one of the fathers from Beau's school called to tell me about something inappropriate my he had done. My son was about seven years old—old enough to know that he shouldn't have done what he did. I was mortified and ashamed. I hate to admit it, but one of my first thoughts was about how poorly this reflected upon me as a parent.

I was walking into the elementary school to pick up my son as I wrapped up the call. My heart was racing, and my pace sped up to match it. I was about to unload my disappointment on him. But just before I saw my boy, I felt a gentle nudge in my heart: *He is already filled with shame. If you come down on him out of your anger, you will lose his heart.*

I came to a screeching halt and paused to regroup and reset. I took a minute to remember who my son was and what he needed from me most in that moment. I knew the answer wasn't judgment.

I walked into the gym and took his little hand in mine as usual as we made our way to the car. I asked him about his day and did my best to listen. Once we got near the car, I squatted down and said, "Jeff called me today and—" Before I could finish the sentence, my sweet Beau burst out in tears and started shaking. The only words that he could mutter were, "I'm so frustrated!" Maybe that was the only way he could put it in the midst of his inner turmoil. He *was* frustrated—frustrated at his decision and with how he had let himself and others down, I suppose.

I looked him square in the eyes and said, "I know who you are, and what you did today is not who you are. I love you and I forgive you." He collapsed in my arms, and we hugged for a very, very, *very* long time. I watched the shame roll away along with his tears.

That night Julie and I took him over to the family's house, where he apologized for what he had done while keeping his head held high. The family was extremely forgiving and gracious as well. We wanted him to take responsibility without the shame and guilt. Removing the weight we put on one another is as difficult as trying to get Gorilla Glue off our fingertips. It takes a lot of time and creates a lot of pain.

Julie and I spend a lot of time discussing the topic of identity: who we are as human beings and how we live our lives based upon that. Brené Brown has done extensive work around the subject of shame, which has skyrocketed her to international acclaim. One of the takeaways of her work is that shame says, "I *am* bad," whereas guilt says, "I've *done* something bad." We believe that behaviors can be a reflection of one's identity, but they do not define a person.

We refuse to let our kids believe that that they should be defined by their worst choices. We teach them about their worth and hold them accountable for their decisions, but we will not allow them to live from a place of shame. If my son had believed that his mistake was *who* he was, then his expectation of himself would be to repeat this behavior, and his future actions would reflect that. As we have built this perspective into our children, we have watched them blossom into young people who live in openness, honesty, and security. And when they make poor choices, they have learned to take responsibility, ask for forgiveness, and move on with a new level of awareness and sensitivity.

That moment with my son became a real marker for us in our parenting. It cemented for me the power of forgiveness and underlined the freedom it brings when we give it to ourselves. Beau released himself from that shame and walked into who he really is by taking responsibility and apologizing. He grew up a lot in that moment. That is the goal; that's what we all long to be able to give one another. Yet how many times have parents said the words "shame on you" to their children after they make poor decisions? Those words are more powerful and soul-crippling than you may realize. Many times when our kids have made poor choices, Julie and I have had to pause and do some soul-searching before reacting. Our reactions as parents can come from our own lingering shame or fear from our childhood traumas. We have to pivot away from this kind of destructive language and keep turning ourselves toward something richer and more transformative.

Viktor Frankl, who survived four Nazi concentration camps during WWII and authored the masterpiece *Man's Search For Meaning*, wrote that "each of us has his own inner concentration camp . . . we must deal with, with forgiveness and patience—as full human beings; as we are and what we will become."[1] Frankl was in an actual, inescapable prison, being taunted daily by fear, intimidation, and oftentimes torture. Yet he became a free man, in his words, not when he was released from the cruel camp but when he allowed forgiveness to work its way into his heart.

Achieving growth in a particular virtue, such as patience, kindness, or generosity, doesn't happen by osmosis; it happens through opportunity. People will test and challenge the strength and resolve of these virtues in our lives. The virtue of forgiveness is no exception, but it hits at the deepest parts of the human heart.

When I try to distill the essence of what creates the desire to forgive, I find it's hard to do. Is it grace, empathy, time, counseling? While those can be pieces that help us move toward forgiveness, I think there is something greater that is the actual key that unlocks the fortified, barricaded, triple-enforced safe called *forgiveness*. I believe it is love. Not flippant, weak, and sappy love that comes and goes, but gritty love.

Julie and I have chosen to be guided as a family by a Bible verse found in 1 Peter: "Above all, love each other deeply, because love covers over a multitude of sins" (4:8). There is a love that can reach beyond what seems reasonable, fair, and right to cover over bleeding hearts. A love able to dispense a canopy of grace where it is completely unmerited. I know this because I have experienced it in my own life in a way that seemed impossible. This love that I'm speaking about is hard to describe but comes from some-where—or, I should say, someone. God is love. It's his essence, not just one of his traits. Everything about God is love, and when we tap into that, we have struck gold.

The power of forgiveness is backed up by scientific research. One article noted that "scientists who study forgiveness have long agreed that it is one of the most important contributors to a healthy relationship," and "people who practice unconditional forgiveness are more likely to enjoy longer lives."[2] Forgiveness can possibly extend your life! The article continued: "Couples who practice forgiveness are more likely to enjoy longer, more satisfying romantic relationships."[3] Our souls long to be given the chance to love deeply, to forgive huge debts, to watch one another overcome our own worst selves, and see change. And we know that forgiveness happens best in families.

Forgiveness is the first step after betrayal, frustration, or even the smallest slight. It's also the second step and the third. And depending on the severity of the wound, it is likely something that we have to revisit for the rest of our lives. Forgiveness is the filter of our emotions. We need to let ourselves be people who make both small and large mistakes—releasing ourselves from judgment and condemnation, learning to move on and turn toward a higher goal with each failure. Once we learn to forgive ourselves, it is much easier for us to extend forgiveness to others.

(Julie)

Every Chance You Get

When Chris and I have mishandled a situation with our children, overreacted to an issue, or hurt them with our words, we model the practice of looking our kids in the eyes and saying, "I was wrong when I said _____. I was feeling _____." Or "I was speaking from my own issue of _____. Will you please forgive me?" And when one of the kids does something harmful or hurtful to a sibling or parent, we have taught them to take responsibility for their actions and apologize without shame. If they aren't ready to apologize or choose forgiveness in that moment, we give them the time and space they need to work through their anger until they are. You can't force forgiveness because it is a willful choice of the heart. Sincerity is key. But when they are ready, they hug it out and move on with life.

We can say the following without any reservation: we have experienced the greatest intimacy with another person when there is genuine repentance and forgiveness on both sides. The process removes the distance. It doesn't mess around in the past. This daily practice is about moving toward a future without burdens.

Forgiveness can lead to lasting intimacy, but it doesn't *need* to. The main goal of forgiveness isn't to keep something but to release it. Bitterness, pain, frustration, judgment—the goal is to flush these emotions out of our bodies and minds. Forgiveness is the gateway to healing, but healing takes time.

What do you do when someone has genuinely betrayed you in a way that feels like you cannot come up for air? Do *you* believe forgiveness and restoration is even possible?

Well, we *know* that it is.

(Chris)

The Unraveling

The day I discovered that Julie had been unfaithful to me was the hardest day of my life. We hadn't been married long. I had come home early that day and gone to the mailbox, where I opened up the overly stuffed envelope with our phone bill. As I looked over the pages—which I didn't usually do—I saw a pattern. A number of incoming and outgoing calls at odd times of the day was listed, page after page, to and a from a person who was no stranger to me. I felt nauseated and weak at the knees. I knew that my life was never going to be the same. The news not only rocked my world but shook the core of my identity.

Thoughts swirled in my mind: *What's wrong with me? Why wasn't I enough? What will I do now?* Oh, and, *I am a pastor. What if everyone at church finds out? Who's going to want to follow me?* That last one may sound a bit shallow, but I was twenty-four years old. I couldn't help but wrestle with the sense that my whole life, career, and future were unraveling, and I didn't know how to make it stop.

I confronted Julie, and she immediately admitted my worst fear. She was heartbroken, full of remorse and shame. When I looked into her eyes, I could see she felt lost. I had to leave the conversation. I didn't know where I would go, but I grabbed my Bible and I started to drive, tears flowing, my heart pounding and mind racing in disbelief.

I didn't get very far down the road before I whipped into a coffee shop right off the highway and walked inside. I didn't know whom to call. I was the leader; I didn't feel I had a trusted person to reach out to. I felt completely alone and scared out of my mind. I ordered a coffee and sat down at a table for two.

Desperate, I told God that I was lost and didn't know what to do. I dropped my jumbo-size Life Application Study Bible that I had used since high school on the shiny brown table. I didn't flip through it; I dropped it. When I looked down, I did a double take. The first verse I saw was Hosea 3:1:

The LORD said to me, "Go, show your love to your wife again, though she is loved by another man and is an adulteress. Love her as the LORD loves the Israelites."

Underneath that scripture was Julie's signature, dated three years earlier, when we were dating. To this day she has no recollection of ever signing my Bible, but regardless of how her signature got there, it became a thread of hope. I felt God speak to my pounding heart: *If you love and forgive Julie like I have, I'll heal your marriage.*

It was supernatural and unexplainable, beyond anything that I have ever experienced. Because my heart was open to releasing Julie from judgment, I felt God pouring out a deep love for Julie and the other person involved in a way that enabled me to forgive without hesitation.

I am hesitant to share this story because I do not want to sound like a saint. I'm not. I'm just as capable of letting bitterness reside in me as anybody else. I believe that when something like this happens in intimate relationships, there is so much space for each person to choose how they will respond. A lot of factors contributed to our healing: we were young, I was just discovering the stories of Julie's past wounds, and we were both committed to change. Reconciliation doesn't have to be the outcome of an affair. Hear me when I say that we know forgiveness doesn't always mean remaining in relationship. Julie and I intentionally support our friends who have chosen divorce instead. Yet I am offering this part of our story to show you that you *can* heal even the deepest wounds, and do so in a way that you never imagined, if you both choose forgiveness and restoration.

I am also not implying that this is possible only for Christians, because I know many people who have done the hard work of counseling and therapy and come to a place of closure and forgiveness. But for me, my faith in God and my understanding of God's love was pivotal in choosing to reconcile my marriage.

I don't want to give you the idea that forgiveness is my super-power, but I can say that the day my world came apart, I made a willful decision that I would not be bitter and rot. The aftermath, however, wasn't so easy to untangle. Julie and I were in ministry work together, pouring our lives into the young people in our community who needed an example of a healthy marriage. I forgave her that day, and the next day, and for many days after that. I met with the other person involved and told him that I forgave him as well. But even though I was healing, the pain of the betrayal stayed with me for many years.

For me, restoration looked like a lot of prayer, asking God to give me the grace to do what I couldn't do on my own. It also looked like a daily intentional choice to let things go and to choose love over my pain. This meant letting go of bitterness and destructive thought patterns via a concoction of lots of practice, journaling, and counseling. Unfortunately, pain is not something written in pencil you can just casually erase because you want to choose love. I found that love and pain worked in tandem to a newly formed rhythm in a long journey to forge something more whole.

While I was able to release Julie from guilt in my heart, it took years to be able to fully move on in my mind and for our trust to be rebuilt. There were many mornings when I would wake up and feel angry. My imagination would run away from me, and I would have to stop and remind myself who Julie was, how one set of choices didn't define the whole of her. Sometimes I just needed to cry. It took many months for me to finally reach out to a friend who I trusted and unload it all.

Forgiveness is a process because the memory of the betrayal never fully goes away; it leaves a scar. I often wonder whether I ever allowed myself to really grieve. I don't think that I did. I was young, and grief wasn't something I was familiar with or encouraged to acknowledge. Now, decades later, I wish I had given myself space to grieve following Julie's confession.

I have discovered both the unpredictability and the necessity of grief. The grieving process doesn't entail shortcuts or follow a formula; it's different for everyone. There were several years when that wound felt so incredibly tender that it could take me out at any moment.

Julie's choices impacted our entire lives. We ended up leaving the people we loved and the little church in Lorena, Texas, that we'd served at since we got married, to heal in a new place. We took the house our relationship had built down to the studs so that we could rebuild our marriage.

A good indicator of whether we have truly forgiven someone is when we are able to separate what they did from who they are. I know Julie. I can see when a broken pattern or piece of her past is affecting her despite her desire to act differently. I know when her behavior doesn't line up with her intention. Our marriage counselor even told her, "Julie, you are dangerously righteous." He hit the nail on the head! The counselor helped her to separate her decision from her identity. This didn't excuse or gloss over the pain she caused; it helped her climb out of the pit of shame and guilt and believe that she was still worthy of love and relationship. He helped her get to the root of the issues in her past that contributed to her decision.

(Julie)

Being Forgiven

You feel terrible when your betrayal is brought to light, but not as bad as the one who was on the receiving end of your screwup. But being caught was the beginning of our healing, of making really hard choices to work through it. To stay. To wrestle with the emotions. And for me, to wonder if I could receive Chris's forgiveness, even though it felt so undeserved.

As Chris shared, he chose to forgive before I had even earned back his trust. It's hard for me to wrap my mind around that. I was the one who betrayed him, who created the wound, the heartache. To this day, the process of receiving forgiveness and working toward healing is the hardest thing I've ever had to wrestle with. More than lost friendships, abuse, and even cancer, my choice to have an affair was a bulldozer that shattered so many pieces of our home that it seemed impossible to repair. My shame was everywhere—and as we've discussed, shame shouts the loudest, stings the hardest, and punches you in the gut so hard that you wonder if the air will ever come back into your lungs. Chris forgave me, but I remained ashamed.

Honestly, at the time, I kind of wanted the easier solution: Chris would give me what I deserved and leave me, and then we could move on. I guess I thought divorce would be a way to accept that I sucked as a human. I could just hold on to my pain and wallow in self-pity (which is just another form of pride) rather than address what had led me to make the choices I did. My insides screamed, *Please don't make me pull off the mask that keeps me safe—I don't want to look at the person underneath it!* I wanted so badly to blame my choice on these broken parts of myself. Strangely, it made me think I would feel better. But how selfish it was. Shame is selfish, even though we can convince ourselves it protects us. Pain desperately wants to blame. It feels easier to defend our undeniably wrong choices (even subtly) than to actually do the work to heal, to rebuild, to unwrap what led to our poor choices.

The torment of my shame was the heaviest consequence I felt after Chris confronted me. I had lived more than a decade in a daily struggle to love myself. I had so much hidden pain. I never knew how deeply fragmented I was until the aftermath of the affair. All I could do was tell myself that I was broken and had unresolved pain. I needed some excuse to ease my own unraveling.

I didn't know how to fully receive Chris's forgiveness because I couldn't forgive myself. I walked through life bent over from the weight of shame for quite a long time. But I didn't give up—and Chris certainly didn't. The million little choices of humility, vulnerability, therapy, and letting myself be undone over and over again slowly helped me walk upright again.

Receiving Chris's forgiveness was key in rebuilding our trust. I wish I could offer you a simple solution to help you forgive yourself once and for all, but I don't. It doesn't exist. I have to make the choice every day to forgive the parts of me that wreak havoc on my self-perception in my roles as a parent, coworker, daughter, friend, and wife.

I had to stop making excuses for the pain I caused. My decision to seek healing was what helped Chris see I was serious about changing, about learning to see myself in the right way so I could love him well. I was honest about my progress (and our progress as a couple), or the lack thereof. I was carrying so much anger: at myself, at Chris, at the man I was involved with, and then back at me again. I felt a constant whiplash of emotions. But let me tell you something that still moves me to tears: Chris held on tight to me. He fought for me. He reminded me of what he saw in me and believed about me despite my poor choices. Was that always easy for him? No way. I guarantee he didn't always like me in the process. But it was pure. It was authentic. And his sincere love kept me moving forward little by little.

(Chris)

Starting Over

Forgiveness can act like a defibrillator in a lifeless relationship. Our marriage was seemingly dead. We had some deep pain and broken patterns in how we had begun our life together, and we took responsibility for that. Forgiveness allowed breath to come back in and life to be restored. Now we are not just married but tethered together; our relationship is stronger than ever. We have both come to the conclusion that, as painful as it was, we wouldn't go back and change our story.

When there is true forgiveness, the past is not something to bring up as blackmail in a conflict.

(Julie)

The Cement of Life

Henri Nouwen wrote, "Forgiveness is the cement of community life. Forgiveness holds us all together through good and bad times, and it allows us to grow in mutual love."[4] I like to think about this in regards to humanity as a whole. I truly believe that at our core we want to be there for others, yet our own needs might conflict and interfere with our desire to show up, to give, to support. We are not always able to give or receive the love each of us needs and deserves in our daily lives because of our natural limitations. Our love has limits.

Let's talk about the stench of bitterness that can come from a lack of forgiveness. Gosh, it reeks. I've had an ongoing tussle with bitterness these last few years. It's crept up mainly from relationships but also around politics and religion. Bitterness is its own cancer that usually ends in death—death of relationships and eventually the death of love. Have you ever met a person who lives in the past and constantly recounts the ways they have been hurt by others? It's like tires spinning in the mud. Lots of energy being spent but no movement forward. And it kicks up mud on those around them.

What I've learned in this season is that forgiving those who have hurt us is a gift we give to ourselves. Like priests in a Catholic confessional, we must tell ourselves, *I am forgiven*, and regarding those who hurt us, *You are forgiven*. If you are ruminating over who has wronged you, licking your wounds and waiting for an

175

apology, you will likely never move forward. When you behave like this, it's as if you have given the offender the keys to your jail cell, not realizing that you can take back the keys, unlock your own door, and step out into freedom.

The greatest measure of freedom from bitterness is when we can bless others and actually wish them well. Again, this doesn't mean you have to be in a relationship with them, but that you have your heart in a place that you want no harm to come to them. Please, give yourself a heaping spoonful of grace if you aren't there yet. There is no timeline on this journey of forgiveness, and certainly no room for a satchel of guilt and regret to accompany you.

Daily Bread: The Practice

The opportunities to practice forgiveness are endless. The person who stole your parking space. Your child who has lost their seventh water bottle at school. The waitress who messed up your order for the second time. Or your dog, who thought it was a good idea to throw up on your new rug. Let it go, let it go, and let it go again. A forgiving person is light, hopeful, present, kind, and free. That's the kind of person I aspire to be.

Chris and I don't consider unforgiveness an option. Forgiveness is our daily bread, and it's the centerpiece of so many people's faith practices. I might feel like I don't *want* to extend forgiveness, but I *will*, eventually. No matter how hard it is or how long it takes, we must choose to make this a part of our lives so that we can move forward.

More than twenty years ago, I looked my abuser in the eye and forgave him. It didn't mean I liked him; it didn't mean I trusted him or wanted to be his friend. No way. But what it did do was release me from this sense of power he had over me. I forgave him for me. However, this is *my* story of abuse and healing, and this is what worked for me. Trauma is complicated, and I'm not suggesting you have to give forgiveness in the way I chose. But my experience was that this face-to-face act of forgiveness changed me.

Bitterness and resentment can dam up your life. Imagine rocks, tree limbs, and debris piling up in a stream; over time, the flow will stop. That is what happens to our hearts when we are unwilling to forgive. We find ourselves defined by our offense, our anger, even our self-hatred. Forgiveness liberates.

Release

Most of us have a relationship that feels unresolved, and it hurts. Perhaps you have tried to have a conversation for reconciliation that wasn't reciprocated. Reconciliation can't be forced, so the relationship remains in a state of uncertainty. We must fight to keep our hearts in a place of peace, choosing again and again to absolve the other person of their wrongdoing. Let us offer a few suggestions in pursuit of practicing forgiveness:

- At the end of the day, spend a few moments in meditation. Scan your day, and let go of any hurtful or negative interactions that you experienced.
- Make letting go of resentful or bitter emotions a daily habit—through journaling, prayer, or body movements (breath work)—that will help lead you to forgiveness.
- If you find yourself in a situation where you are unable to forgive, consider reaching out to a spiritual mentor or counselor for help working through the pain.

You can do it. You can be free.

Chapter 9

Service with a Smile

*The best way to find yourself is to lose
yourself in the service of others.*
—MAHATMA GANDHI

(Julie)

The Sweetest Things

Nothing is better than that month of the year when I wake up
to the smell of balsam pine. The whimsical greens and reds
sprinkled in my living room set a serious mood. At my house, my
eyes are first drawn to the celebratory, pink "cancer free" tree
that sits on the piano, giving me chills when I see it and evok-
ing both a settled happiness and a searing pain. I always take a
moment to reminisce at the family tree filled with my children's
handmade ornaments and laminated pictures of their innocent

faces sprinkled with glitter and held by pieces of yarn. The mantel looks almost proud to be shouldering the sacred stockings with the embroidered names *Beau*, *Nate*, *Brooks*, and *Joy*. I light a fire and sit in my yellow crushed-velvet chair, savoring the morning hours as the twinkling lights lull me into joy and gratitude for what is all around me. I reflect on how thankful I am to be alive and how I have been forever changed by those who have cared so deeply for me.

One December, right after starting my very first round of chemo, we were shoehorned into a little Airbnb. There was no room to put up a tree, and our stockings were buried away in our storage unit in Oklahoma. My GG friends delivered a bundle of packages—including a mini–Christmas tree and stockings for each of our kids—to help our temporary house feel like home. I can still see the utter excitement on Joy's and Brooks's faces as they sifted through all the holiday gifts and decorations while watching *Elf* for the 143rd time. The tiny tree with mini lights made everything a little lighter, a little less hard. Those gifts reminded us of how holiday magic makes us feel warm and held. We needed anything and everything that could made us feel that way.

Being served by my closest friends and even strangers during my illness opened a doorway to healing I didn't know I needed—or that our family needed. The gift of serving is a precious thing.

In the context of a family unit—and by *family*, we mean a group of people who choose one another—a culture of service and of sharing what you have is what makes it all work. Knowing you have gifts and ideas to offer is important, but consistently showing up in the lives of those you love with a readiness to help?

That's something even richer. When every member sees themselves as a contributor and not a consumer, there is a greater sense of purpose and unity.

A culture of service also prevents the situation where one person becomes the designated workhorse of the group. In our communities, our friendships, and our families, our goal must always be to create equilibrium. Balance. No one holds power over another. There can't be a default "servant" who will slip back into the kitchen during the meal to start tidying up the chaos while everyone else enjoys dessert. We love to say to those people things like, "You have such a servant's heart." We can even *praise* this unequal ground, reinforcing a status quo in which most of us don't have to do the grunt work and the faithful few slave away for the applause they may get when we are all going home. It's not right, but we have all experienced this dynamic, either as the silently frustrated person doing all the work or the chill patron.

I have seen that play out with my kids and even Chris and me in simple, mundane tasks. For example, someone sees that the trash needs to be taken out, but they pass it by because Beau always does it. Or if Brooks takes Champ on a walk five days in a row, his siblings assume they are off the hook for this chore, subtly shrugging it off under the guise of "Brooks obviously likes to do it." Eventually, these unequal dynamics blow up, so we must cut them off before they do. The "silent servants" in the hierarchy never stay that way—nor should they.

There is only one way to ensure this doesn't happen: *everyone serves*.

When everyone brings their gifts and a willingness to serve

for the good of those around them, it's like the combination of lots of ingredients that, together, make an irresistible treat.

Do you remember our family mission statement that we shared earlier? "We are a joyful family. We love Jesus, we serve each other, and we honor everyone." Out of these sixteen words, four have proved to be the hardest to live by: "We serve each other." To be honest, we aren't always great at this.

Serving has to come from a place of love. If I tell one of my kids, "Clean up your brother's room or you're grounded," I could force them into serving. But giving of yourself carries potency when it is done by choice, in love. Sure, some of us are naturally wired to just do the things that need to be done, and do them with a happy heart. But then there are those who respond to a request to serve as though you've strapped them down and threatened them with only eating veggies the rest of their life.

Yet choosing service does something to us intrinsically. It opens our eyes to see and appreciate each person's unique contributions. It's a wild thing, but every time we have "helped" someone, as a family or individually, we have seen the tables turn, and we learn something. Even the act of serving others brings an opportunity for real connection. Every person who has come to live at our house over the years has brought something to the table that was beautiful and something that was hard. But the thing is, up front we don't ever know which will outweigh the other.

Chris and I invited a young woman named Lacey to live with us when Beau and Nate were really young. She came from a background of extensive abuse followed by tormenting thoughts of taking her own life. When we met her, she couldn't look us in the eyes, and she suffered from what we came to call "episodes," where she would black out as if unconscious for hours at time. When a friend introduced us to her, I immediately signed up to help—not as a project manager but as a friend, a support.

From the beginning, having her in our home was more than we had anticipated. I'll never forget the first night we woke up to her screaming. I ran into her room in case she was being assaulted, only to discover that she suffered night terrors from PTSD. These became common occurrences.

She also had uncontrollable fits of rage and self-harm, all while our two little boys were tucked into their bunk beds next door. Once we had to pull her out of the bathtub, where she had passed out and nearly drowned, and we had more than a dozen trips to the ER from times she had unexplainably fallen and hurt herself. One time, I had taken her to a counseling session, and I watched as she stubbornly left in the middle, stomping out in her tattered Chuck Taylors, walking nine miles without her phone. I spent the whole night driving around town to try to find her. She eventually came home that next day, and after the tightest hug I could manage, I sent her to her room. Can you send someone only nine years younger than you to their room? Well, I did. I was so angry—and relieved.

(Chris)

Saying Yes to People Is Saying Yes to Service

When we say yes to someone becoming family, we say yes to the baggage that they bring with them. As Julie said, we questioned our decision to bring Lacey into our home. We even had well-meaning people tell us we were in way over our heads. I'll admit that there were times that we said yes to too much and took on more than we should have. We tried to fix things we couldn't and heal wounds we weren't privy to treat.

Lacey lived with us for nearly five years in three different cities. When we moved, she moved with us. She was a consistent part of our family. Over the years, we got to know who she really was. The healthier she became, the more of her gifting and brilliance would shine. She was resilient and unflappable, a dynamic administrator with an eye for order. In Lacey, my kids received a big sister, and Julie and I received a sort of older daughter and then, later, a dear friend.

It may be that our attempts at providing family for Lacey changed her life, but she changed ours as well. We still get watery-eyed every Christmas when we come across her stocking, which used to hang on the mantel right next to our kids'. Thankfully, she grew to a place where she could move out and move on with her life. She is now married, successful, and happy, and I can't imagine not having her as a part of our story.

We share this example of Lacey because we went into the relationship expecting to serve her. And we did. But she also served us by meeting practical needs for our family. She would cook us incredible meals and drop off the kids at school. She helped us organize our home to run more efficiently and truly became part of the family. We wouldn't want it any other way.

Service Is a Posture of Heart

When Julie and I were first dating, we spent our summer days going door-to-door in the trailer park of Lorena, working with a handful of youth to help residents with a variety of outdoor chores and maintenance. This little town, with a population of 1,764, taught us the untainted joy of service with no strings attached.

We didn't have much to offer other than a ragtag bunch of youth with some paintbrushes and rickety lawn mowers. We came with no agenda other than to do something for the residents that would ease their burden. Our students fell in love with the joy they could bring people through the simple act of mowing lawns or painting trim, and we all learned that when serving is about giving, we often receive more than we give. No kidding—I received a Facebook message just a few weeks ago from a lady who we met at the trailer park more than twenty years ago, thanking us for the impact we had made on her!

Selfless service changes hearts. It requires that we check some of our less-than-desirable emotions—jealousy, frustration, impatience, pride—at the door. Serving can sometimes be hard and inconvenient because it requires a heart posture of giving. It costs us something extra, but the sacrifice bends us. It's disruptive. This may be incovenient, but it pays incredible dividends in return. In other words, sacrifice is essential. It is not a one-off event but a daily activity—a by-product of humility.

There are so many ways to serve one another. As parents, it looks like making sure that our kids have everything they need to thrive. We stay up late to help them with projects, and we wake up early to shuttle them to sports or music practice. As friends and neighbors, it means finding moments to step in and make life a little easier for someone else. We have a friend who has the time-consuming position of vice president of a private university, yet I have watched him show up week after week just as the sun is rising on Sunday mornings to unload our storage shed for the church and meticulously arrange the folding chairs in our undersized school cafetorium (cafeteria + auditorium). One of our neighbors sometimes offers to walk our dog or pick up one of our kids when we cannot.

To be honest, I struggle with grumbling when I am asked or expected to do something beyond my comfort level or that invades my time. I can't think of a time I actually enjoyed helping someone load and unload a U-Haul trailer or cleaning up after a party. I do it, but not always joyfully. These "inconveniences" have become opportunities to get over myself and serve others, and I've never regretted helping out. I've been grateful.

Serving is a two-sided coin. We sometimes have to choose to attend to our own needs before we are healthy enough to attend to the needs of others. Right now, Julie's focus is on serving herself. If you asked her to host an event, organize a meal train, or babysit, she may say no because having firm boundaries while she heals from post-traumatic stress disorder as a result of her cancer journey is her priority. She has to be more selective about when she says yes. The boundaries that she is learning are what will allow her to serve with greater capacity in the next season. We must extend grace to others when their service doesn't look like what we need or expect. We must even extend that grace to ourselves when we just aren't able to show up the way we might under other circumstances.

Julie and I long to build a way of life that unflinchingly provides out of deep, authentic love. We long to truly prefer others over ourselves. I wish I could say that we have served as much as we have been served, but we've been mostly on the receiving end, which has been an incredible lesson for us.

Service doesn't always have to take the form of a big thing; rather, it can look like the *right* thing needed at that time. Our trusty next-door neighbor, Michael Paul, always has exactly what we need to borrow and brings it over at a moment's notice: a ladder, a table, a shovel, a cup of sugar, or a printer for a last-minute book report. Michael Paul is *there*. He has taught me so much about serving through his constant willingness to give a hand wherever needed without thinking twice. It's not rocket science, but the decision to just be there for each other changes our lives.

(Julie)

People Before Projects

Chris and I have to remind ourselves that *love* means "people before projects." A few weeks ago, our neighbor Dorothy frantically called Chris after accidentally locking herself out of her house. Dorothy was widowed a couple of years ago and now lives alone. Chris was smack-dab in the middle of a house project when she called. The timing was inconvenient. But Chris came over and scaled her wooden fence, nearly split his skinny jeans, and stuck his long arm up the tiny doggy door to unlock the side door. Dorothy was beyond grateful, and I think Chris felt kind of cool, like he had saved the day.

The next day we came home to a dozen tea cakes from Martino's Bakery in Burbank. They are his favorite dessert, and he thoroughly enjoyed them. But more than that, those little exchanges ended up bringing us closer to Dorothy. By saying yes to serving, we keep redirecting our hearts toward who we want to be—not just to our neighbors but to those closest to us.

I recently saw the brilliant movie *A Man Called Otto*, featuring Tom Hanks. Otto is a widower who has lost his will to live. Being the thorough, measured engineer that he is, he meticulously plans his earthly exit, but his first attempt at ending his life fails. Moments before his second try, he hears a knock at the door. His bubbly new neighbor, Marisol, has cooked a meal for him. Marisol and her little family make it their mission to win over Otto by their selfless love. His hard shell slowly begins to soften, and these strangers form an unlikely family.[1] Serving without expectation, just to love, is a powerful force.

That "Secret Sauce"

An article on Psychology Today states, "Research has found many examples of how doing good, in ways big or small, not only *feels* good, but also *does* us good. For instance, the well-being-boosting and depression-lowering benefits of volunteering have been repeatedly documented. As has the sense of meaning and purpose that often accompanies altruistic behavior."[2] Yep, serving does a body good! Scrubbing your pregnant friend's kitchen floor, doing your parents' dishes while chatting with them, or driving your person to the airport in five o'clock traffic pays dividends.

When you're moving houses and nobody shows to help you lift your stuff into the moving truck, you don't feel loved no matter how many texts of affirmation you get that day. We need each other, not just emotionally but physically. We need each other to open doors for us when our hands are full. To stoop down and pick up a dropped item. To show up early to a party to help set up. When someone meets our needs, it opens our hearts. Those memories imprint.

When we were moving like nomads around LA—in the middle of my doctor appointments, me throwing up, and my hair falling out—we were constantly blown away by the friends who showed up for us. Nate and Sarah allowed us to use us their master bedroom one evening when we had nowhere to go the night before I started my fifth round of chemo. Chris had to fly out of town for three days, and my Katy drove over five hours after work that evening to stay with us. Then that same week, Lindsay (our neighbor from Oklahoma whose daughter was Joy's closest friend) called and said, "What can I do? I want to do something!" I didn't know exactly what I needed; I was so overwhelmed. So she got on a plane to LA to get Joy and then flew back to Oklahoma with her for a couple of weeks. It was right when Joy was struggling the most and needed something familiar.

My oldest brother left his family for a weekend to come help me during my treatments. He bought all the groceries, cooked every meal, and (most profoundly) cleaned my toilets. And my parents, whew, where do I begin with the ways they effortlessly cared for our family? That would need a whole chapter on its own.

Bottom line, when we are joyfully served by others, it's like eating the most decadent chocolate cake on fine china. During my illness, the sweets kept coming.

Family doesn't function well without servanthood in the mix. During the hardest moments of my suffering, other peoples' actions spoke to me of my worth. I want my actions to do the same for them.

(Chris)

Service Keeps Us Alive

As we give of ourselves, we find out something deep and secret: *we're made for this kind of love.* The more we decide to value assisting others, the more we feel the truth of this statement. The gifts we have been given exist for the good of others, and they are meant to be given away. Hoarding our gifts feels unnatural, even unhealthy. Consumer culture has lured us into an entitlement mentality that tells us that the more we have, the happier we will be. I think in some ways, we have all swallowed that lie—hook, line, and sinker.

The Dead Sea is a salt lake located in the Jordan Rift Valley. The salt content is so high that the human body can easily float in it. Yet as a result of the salinity, the lake cannot sustain life. In fact, nothing lives in the Dead Sea, hence the name. Just north of the Dead Sea is the Sea of Galilee. And while both the Sea of

Galilee and the Dead Sea receive their water from the Jordan River, and though they are located in the same region, they couldn't be more different. The Sea of Galilee is filled with beauty and boundless life, including more than twenty different types of fish. So what's the difference? The Jordan River seamlessly flows in and out of the Sea of Galilee, but the Dead Sea is below sea level and has no outlet. It is estimated that over seven million tons of water evaporate from the Dead Sea every day.[3] It is able to take in but incapable of giving out.

I'm sure you can see where I'm going with this. When we live our lives with the primary purpose of receiving and do not create streams that allow us to give, we become dead on the inside. If humility is the seedbed of growth, forgiveness tills the ground and giving is the fertilizer. Too many people spend their lives looking for what they can receive and not what they can give.

I've learned a lot about this from Jules. I like to be comfortable and am a high-functioning homebody. I like nice hotels, clean clothes, great coffee, and tasty food. I'd rather sit down over coffee with a person in need then paint a faded wall in hundred-degree heat. Julie is an extravagant giver and has pushed me and our family beyond our comfort level. We are on a path to growth, and Julie and I, along with our kids, are working to be aware of what we are good at, and to live as people who give our gifts away freely, without expectations.

Pops (Julie's dad) is so good at this. He is an expert balloon maker, a below-average magician, and a professional extrovert. For years now we've loved watching how he has worked along-side Annie B (my mother-in-law) with an organization called

Whiz Kids, which provides mentorship and tutoring to disadvantaged children. They have consistently gone above and beyond the allotted one hour per week of service and become extended family to many of their mentees. That encouragement has inspired them to keep serving and pulling in other friends to do the same.

Our friend Pamela, who is an incredible woman and a single mom, was part of our community in Oklahoma. She worked long hours at Walmart to pay the bills but spent her spare time and change baking extravagant cakes. She even made me a three-tier cake for my fortieth birthday party. She was humbling to watch, and her cakes were amazing to eat.

Giving is full of gentle reminders of life's fragility and the absolute wonder of how multifaceted the human race really is. Rich or poor, well-fed or hungry, from the unschooled to the ones who have every advantage, everyone has the opportunity to make a substantial difference in the lives of others. Giving says more about the giver than anyone else, and in this world there are shining stars everywhere.

(Julie)

Sincerity on Display

I shared earlier in the book how my girls' group (GG) supported me on my cancer journeys in 2018 and 2021. I saw firsthand the radical ways these women, who barely knew me at the time, could carry what was a real beat-up Julie down to a safe basecamp to recover. To regroup. To feel. I was in a new place, far from our dear friends who lived next door on the cul-de-sac in Norman, feeling as naked and vulnerable on the inside as I ever remember feeling—and they just held me. They climbed the mountain of family for me.

These women and their families (get ready for a long list) brought me meals, binge-watched Netflix with me (when I was so sick from chemo, I would pop CBD gummies while eating insane amounts of thin crust pizza), and cleaned my toilets. They took me to the ER, brought *more* meals, prayed incessantly over me, threw me surprise parties, and redecorated my whole room while I was out of the country receiving cancer treatments. They didn't do all that to fill a need in themselves. They did it out of sincere love. And in most circumstances, I had nothing to give back. They honored me. They called me worthy just because I am.

I have had the joy of watching Chris gain some of the deepest, most sincere friendships of his life since moving to LA. Tim became his voice of truth when Chris couldn't see straight as we bounced from house to house. Over the last four years, they have exchanged hundreds of video messages that became like counseling for Chris. Ben showed up seemingly out of nowhere when he heard about Chris's dream of creating TV show ideas that would inspire and bring people together. They became not only business partners but close friends who continue to build and dream together.

We feel lucky and blessed as we know that not everyone has these types of relationships. All that we know is that we would not have made it without these unexpected friends. I have seen this play out as well in our kids' lives. Each of them left behind precious relationships in Oklahoma, and slowly those gaps have been filled, though there were many hard and lonely days for them in between. Through the hardships that our kids have endured, we have watched in amazement at how their love for one another has grown—aside from the times that Brooks wants to throw hands with Beau for beating him in *Fortnite* or Nate wants to move out of their overcrowded room because Brooks is too loud. (Such is life.)

Purpose

Foot washing was once a common practice when entering a home, as sandals left people's feet quite dirty after traveling on endless dusty roads. Jesus took this practical act and turned it into an act of service and humility because "the Son of Man did not come to be served, but to serve" (Matthew 20:28). Rather than his friends washing their own feet, Jesus gently knelt, towel slung around his waist, and began to humbly wash their blistered, filthy feet. Peter, one of Jesus' most devout followers, adamantly objected to this service by his Savior/teacher/master. But Jesus challenged him by declaring that this was an act that he must do and that moving forward, they should do this for others (John 13:1–17). Of course, Jesus wasn't implying that they were to literally wash the stinky feet of strangers but rather take on a posture of servanthood that would require discomfort and denial of their own self-interests.

I'm not sure anyone is born with an innate desire to serve. I actually think the opposite is true. We are born into a me-centered world that caters to the individual. So Chris and I have had to work at providing countercultural situations for our family.

We were on a family vacation a of couple of years ago during one of our many pressing times. The kids were on edge, and their attitudes toward one another were stinky, like their feet. In other words, they were treating each other like crap. So Chris sat them all down in the cozy living room where he had made a crackling fire. He made his way around the room with a large bowl filled with warm water and gently washed the feet of each child, then blotted them dry. It was silent and holy, and the atmosphere shifted. He then asked each of them to wash one another's feet. Without us even asking them to, they began to apologize to one another for their attitudes, and their hearts were soon as clean as their feet.

It's worth doing uncomfortable things—like washing the feet of those we love—to become open to what true love looks like. A friend of ours has been known to go over to someone's house and do a pedicure for them for this very reason; she says that she sees a feeling of dignity come over them as she washes and dries their feet.

A lowly posture isn't a position of dread for Chris and me. It's the centerpiece of joy for our family. And as much as we have tried to encourage an attitude of humility into our little tribe, if the heart is not engaged, serving just becomes another chore or something to check off a list. So when someone suggests or does something that denies them of their own comfort, it's a sign of an engaged heart, of freedom from the tyranny of bondage to self. Purpose infuses each relationship and pushes against the self-centered current of culture that actually leads to less-fulfilled lives.

One of the best things that ever happened to us was not having our own home when we came to LA. Our kids were forced to share not just a room but sometimes a small bed or an air mattress while having their possessions stowed in a faraway storage unit. Simplicity made room for joy that was not based on a feeling but a satisfaction that came from one another's presence. It was a decluttering of the soul, which can then have margin to bless and serve others.

For our relationships to function in a healthy way, this is an essential disposition to have. As Chris and I reflect on the people in our lives who have become family, I see a theme: they each came to us with a desire to bring what they had for the better of all. Service is such a quick entryway into the lives of others. Imagine if we came into relationships with a desire to serve and not to be served. I think we would have a lot more healthy families in the world.

In 2019, I received a call from a stranger who has since become a very special friend in my life. Holly Teixeira, along with her husband, Steve, are the cofounders of 17 Strong, whose mission is to provide "Victory Trips" to young adults age eighteen to forty after they have battled a life-threating illness. The Teixeiras have felt the resounding sting of grief and loss through the death of their son Ryan in 2015, who passed away at the age of twenty from a rare type of cancer. Ryan had hoped and planned for a dream trip with a particular foundation only to find out that he was past the age limit; his trip was denied. Shortly before his passing he launched the nonprofit 17 Strong.

How easy would it have been for Steve and Holly to allow the bitterness of unfulfilled dreams engulf their souls? Instead, they took their sorrow and created a movement that is now giving away all-expense paid vacations to adults who need them. We were blown away when Holly called to tell us that she heard about my cancer journey and wanted to gift us a trip of our dreams. We went on the most amazing trip to the island of Barbados and stayed at an all-inclusive resort, where I ate no less than ten *dozen* gluten-free doughnuts and drank way too many yummy drinks with cute baby umbrellas.

Chris and I had the opportunity to meet with Steve and Holly over lunch and listen to their story. Ryan's last act before dying was one of service, and now numerous individuals are benefiting from it each year.

In spring 2020, shortly after being diagnosed with cancer a second time, I came home from a weekend away with my daughter to find my bedroom repainted and a new, dreamy, camel-stained leather reading chair resting just below two frames etched with my two favorite quotes. Not only that, but there were new bedding and pillows, and our walls had received a long-overdue paint job. My best friends had shown up. They had snuck into the house and taken care of everything—everyone doing what they could, when they could. I broke down sobbing when I walked into the room. My phone blew up that evening with all thirteen women waiting to receive the video of my overwhelmed, undone, overjoyed, sobbing self. Remembering the excitement on their faces and the laughter that it brought still gives me those feelings of being fiercely loved—a gooey, sticky kind of love that can't be washed off easily. When service comes from love, it can give us pure glee. And it wasn't simply about the good deed from my friends; it was that they gave me what I didn't know I needed.

(Chris)

The Best Time

Have you seen a child nearly pee themselves with excitement to give you a picture they worked hard on and made just for you? It's the elation of giving. Yet service has been manipulated in some contexts to be about lacking boundaries—that's not what we are espousing. In fact, I've lived that way before, and it brought me nothing.

When we serve only ourselves, we develop entitlement and a subconscious belief that life is about what we can gain and not what we can give. But in relationships where people give freely, without needing something in return, it's a breath of fresh air, like Pinocchio's joy that "I've got no strings to hold me down." When serving is give-and-take, it becomes about the fun it produces when everyone brings their best.

This is our invitation to you: Give from your abundance, and give from your lack. Step into the powerful flow of seeing what those you love need and helping to supply it. It brings out the best in us all. At the table of honor, we all get to serve.

Make Some Plans

Consider a few ways—from the littlest gesture to the largest act—that you could help someone in your immediate circle. If you are just starting a new friendship, offering to pick them up at the bus stop or checking in to see whether they need help cooking dinner can be a great way to start. Brainstorm and get excited about how your acts might touch the people in your life. Serving has the unrivaled ability to change our perspective and bring us a renewed sense of gratification and joy by focusing on the needs of others.

Find an organization that helps a cause or group of people that you are passionate about, and volunteer with them—either on your own or with your family, housemates, or friends. Maybe you want to help people experiencing homelessness, at-risk mothers and their children, or the prison population. As inconvenient as serving often is, you will always leave with more than you gave. For when we give, we also receive.

Epilogue

Back to Risk

(Julie)

Jane's Song

My cancer diagnosis was crippling in so many ways. Two battles. Twenty-plus rounds of chemotherapy treatment. Radiation. Multiple surgeries. Hair loss, hair regrowth, hair loss again. Twenty moves. Four children. I shudder just typing that. Did that really happen?! Through it all, Chris became the master of *Tetris* suitcase packing into the back of our huge white Suburban and, well, I learned that one can wear the same sweats every day for months on end and still remain married. (Those sweats were given a proper burial just over two years ago. RIP.) Through it all, though, we've learned a better, deeper way to do life than we ever thought was possible. For us, this meant leaving everything that we knew of comfort and stability—family, friends, and our home—to attempt building and creating family in a new place with no security other than each other. Our faith propelled us to step out into the impossible, and God brought amazing people into our lives. Then we made an intentional decision to lean into those relationships and begin to build something together.

I want to tell you about my friend Jane, who went by the stage name Nightbirde. I was gifted her friendship right around the time she had just received the Golden Buzzer from Simon Cowell on *America's Got Talent*. Her inspiring story of her battle with breast cancer, combined with the overnight success of her original song "It's Okay," flipped her life upside down.[1]

Oh, how the world needed to know Jane. We knew each other only for a short six months through texting and video messaging, yet somehow it felt as if I had known her my whole life. We connected for a lot of reasons, but the obvious one was that we both knew what it felt like to have your life derailed by cancer more than once. Cancer is such a thief. I still get a twinge of nausea even typing the ruthless C-word.

Beautiful Jane passed away in February 2022, and my heart aches frequently at the loss of her otherworldly soul. She experienced firsthand the unexpected entanglements and frailty of life—how cancer and success are each their own freight train.

Jane never dissembled her words. I would tell her she was going to beat cancer, that she was just getting started in life, and she would say in her honest, weary way that she was "rebelliously hopeful." And she was. I would sing her a song on voice text and conclude it with a prayer. She would reply honestly, not pretending to be OK when she wasn't, and sharing when she was feeling deeply sad. I cheered her on and even sent her my rainbow-colored wig that she just *had* to have.

Jane supported me, too, in similar ways. On days that I was seeing the world in blacks and grays, she would help me see it in color. When I was weary, she would give me hope in the midst of my sadness. She had this ability to make you feel like you were a part of her family, and her open and frank way of talking brought a sigh of relief to whatever you were going through. Her boundless authenticity proved that although she felt stuck in her body, she was still free.

Her honesty in the struggle of a life being interrupted made me believe I could be honest too. We can be acquainted with grief, physical pain, internal pain, disappointments, anxiety, and the unknown, and still have radiant hope and joy and never give up. Jane showed me what it looks like to bring all the things out from under our rugs. That it truly was OK when the unknowns of life are staring you down. Her life reminded the world that we don't have to be an exact fit in each other's puzzles to experience and fight for family.

(Chris)

Keeping in Step

When we made the move to LA, some of our friends were unable to comprehend our decision. They considered it to be an unfathomable risk that we were taking—with no home, jobs, or income. And then the avalanche of cancer attempted to take us all out. Even when someone's role in your life changes, your love can remain. Family isn't meant to be fickle, but it's not always permanent. I have told my kids many times (and reminded myself) that good people are a gift. Money and things haven't been what we needed most along the journey; it was the people who entered into our story and became family. That's the stuff money can't buy. We have sat our kids down in moments where they were ungrateful or disrespectful, especially toward one another, and given a reminder that at the end of the day, we have each other. And for our little Bennett clan, that will never change because we won't let it. We are fighting for each other every day, even if the connections grow distant.

Our family makes wild choices to walk a mile in one another's shoes. None of us will ever forget the day that we went as a family to the hospital beautician to have Julie's head shaved. As the precious woman, who had shaved hundreds of cancer patients' hair, began to run the blade over Julie's head, something holy happened. I was crying, but all Julie could do was worship. I can't explain it. She was overwhelmed with joy like she had never known in the midst of our sorrow. With tears running down her face and a confounding joy bubbling over, we all cried. The beautician had to stop as she, too, began to cry. She said she had never seen a family be joyful and sorrowful at the same time or watched someone going through so much loss and pain find joy in the middle of it. Though Julie's body was weak and her hair was gone, we were strong; we were together. As I looked at my bald-and-beautiful bride, I knew she couldn't go through this alone. Later that week, the boys and I all decided to shave our heads in solidarity. (After Julie saw me bald, she asked me never to do it again. It's the thought that counts, right?) But I share this story because I want you to know that joy and sorrow can coexist. And with family by your side, you are ready for any fight.

No Regrets

If there's one thing Julie and I have learned, it's that life is short and unpredictable. I stumbled upon a story recently about an Australian palliative care nurse named Bronnie Ware, who cared for patients in the last weeks and months of their lives. She heard a lot of stories, regrets, and epiphanies from her patients. She shared many of them in a blog that eventually became a book titled *The Top Five Regrets of the Dying*. According to Bronnie, one of the top regrets that she heard from patients was the following: "I wish I'd had the courage to live a life true to myself, not the life others expected of me."[2]

Bronnie further explains:

This was the most common regret of all. When people realise that their life is almost over and look back clearly on it, it is easy to see how many dreams have gone unfulfilled. Most people had not honoured even a half of their dreams and had to die knowing that it was due to choices they had made, or not made. Health brings a freedom very few realize, until they no longer have it.[3]

Regret is the rearview mirror of our lives. And while there are lots of things we regret, we rarely have regrets about the risks we have taken. Even the choices Julie and I have made that looked like failures in the eyes of others are now the very things that have propelled us forward. In fact, the opportunity to write this book came about as the result of a "failed" project. We had made a short trailer for a docuseries about becoming family, which was passed along to a publisher. Even though multiple television networks passed on the purchase and production of our show in 2020, that risk has still opened up so many doors for us, including writing this book. We are still taking risks for this dream. Life is too short to play it safe and too exciting to do alone.

That's a Wrap

As we have been writing this book, we are choosing to push past our pastoral tendency to wrap up our message with a bow on top. Instead, we leave it to you, our friendly reader, to work out how to fight for family in your own life. This can feel like a great big experiment at times because family is not a formula. You observe from others, read as much as you can, and then you practice. Isn't it funny and a bit odd that our most intelligent and trained professionals, like doctors and lawyers, still refer to themselves as "practicing"? They have delved deeply enough into their fields to know the truth—that expertise is a myth. None of us in the field of family are professionals. No matter how much we have experienced, we are all practitioners: Experimenting. Failing. Trying again. Failing. Finding some things that work well, then going back to school again to figure out what went wrong.

Remember the themes that we attempted to visit on the daunting mountain of family. Here they are again:

- Honor all.
- Embrace vulnerability.
- Be humble.
- Make boundaries.
- Forgive daily.
- Serve freely.

These values are not meant to be just statements on a wall but daily reminders of the kind of people we want to be—people who build connection in a healthy way. And Julie and I have to *consistently* remind ourselves of them so that we don't get off course. These are the key ingredients to make this family dish, and if one ingredient is missing or the measurements are off, it doesn't quite taste like it's supposed to.

While we were in the final stages of writing this book, our family received a few new opportunities—opportunities that we could take if we moved houses at the end of the summer, during the start of a new football season for Nate the Great. Julie's last surgery, my new job, and the chance for our kids to go to a new school required a lot of rapid decision-making and movement. It was a lot, and the timing would be tough to pull off. We could feel the pressure mounting as we had to move by a certain date or our son would have to miss half of his football season.

Epilogue

So we did what we do, which is "whatever it takes." I drove an hour one way twice a day to get Nate to practice at his new school while Julie packed up our house. (We are really good at that now.) We have learned that you can do almost anything for a season, so we locked in and got it done. Did we embrace the mess as a natural part of life? Hmm, I'm pretty sure we had to, but we hated it. Were we serving everyone? Not exactly. So much of the emphasis was centered on one child that we inevitably and unintentionally neglected the needs of the other kids. Family is a team, and every member is impacted by the decisions we make. Sometimes the group has to make sacrifices for the sake of one of its members. The point is, when the pressure is on, you can see where you've collapsed and where you are still standing. I tell you, Julie under pressure with a house full of boxes was poetry in motion.

The reality is, there is no perfect family, and there is no perfect way to find and experience love. Ultimately, we hope to be able to respond with a yes to the following questions: Did we love those who didn't love us back? Did we forgive and love those who hurt us? Did we give ourselves a break for our failed experiments, and did we practice self-love? Did we choose love over convenience and agreement?

Building connection is about finding joy, but it is still full of peril and uncertainty. We definitely haven't pulled any punches showing that to you, but can you feel how deeply worthwhile we feel all that pain is? This is *the real deal*. This is where you step out into the unknown. Family is the greatest risk you'll ever take. You're betting on the most unpredictable thing you'll ever face:

the human next to you. You're hoping and praying that you get a good return on your investment. But people make choices; they are free agents, and you could be giving up time, money, emotion, and strength for something that won't pan out. The people who disappear. The friends that *can't* go the next mile with you. The end of a marriage. Yet family is still worth fighting for.

Let us take you back to looking up at the mountain range called *family*. The steep, rough, eventful, beautiful climb that we have asked you, in as many ways as we can, to join us on. I can almost imagine you now, staring up your own trek from the base. It's important to not only remember where you are going but to appreciate how far you have come, one shaky step at a time. As you stare at this mountain, you are thinking about that lost relationship, the death of your plans for that "home group" community, the last text that cut you off from your parent. Maybe you are wondering what you'll get if you try again. Let me tell you, we've been there. But here is what just might be up that hill, once you get going: Reconciliation. New beginnings. Personalities you've never interacted with. New jokes and memories. Stories. Deeper connections. Oh, the views and the possibilities are so much greater than the regrets and mistakes.

Friend, we believe in you. We believe you can venture out. You were made to keep going, together, with others.

What is a dream or an adventure that you have always longed to be a part of? What has held you back? It doesn't have to be something as drastic as packing up your life and moving across the country, but there are unfulfilled dreams inside each one of us. There is adventure calling. Maybe your dream looks like learning to play golf or taking that vacation you never got around to. Maybe it's starting a business or writing a book. Whatever your dream is, find family to do it with, and fight for it when it's hard. You will need them—want them—along the way. They may not be writing a book with you or forecasting your financials for your new endeavor, but they will undoubtedly be in your corner for every step. And when you feel that twinge of giving up on this need for belonging, double down and fight not against but *for* this messy and majestic gift called *family*.

Our hunch is that there is a smoking ember inside you that just needs a little breath. Perhaps there is a relationship that you need to move toward or one you need to step away from. Or a brave conversation about past hurt that it's time to unwrap and release. Fortune favors the bold. Maybe you're searching for family, and we hope and believe you will make it. Or maybe you have found your tribe, your clan, your ride-or-dies, your family. Now what? What's next? Maybe it's time to step out and take an adventure so that at the end of your days, you aren't asking, "What if?"

When you look back in twenty years, may you have continued on far enough ahead to say this blessed phrase: "We did it together."

Acknowledgments

To our incredible parents who have unwaveringly loved and supported us along the journey: Thank you for showing us what love and commitment look like.

To our kids and best friends, Beau, Nate, Brooks, and Joy: You are the greatest gift and joy of our lives.

To the countless friends who are like family and have carried us, cried with us, and journeyed with us through it all: This book doesn't exist without you.

Thanks to our fearless agent, Nena Madonia, for taking a risk on us and holding our hand through the entire process: You are forever part of our family.

Acknowledgments

To our loyal friend and brilliant editor, Teresa: Thank you for bringing your literary magic and your whole heart to this book.

To our publisher, Harper Horizon: Thank you for believing in our story and giving us a chance to tell it to the world.

And thank you to Jesus for putting us back together again and again and giving us a story worth sharing.

Finally, to everyone who took the time to read our book: The best is yet to be!

Notes

Introduction

1. Chris Columbus, director, *Harry Potter and the Sorcerer's Stone*, 2001, Burbank, CA: Warner Bros. Pictures.
2. John Leland, "How Loneliness Is Damaging Our Health," *New York Times*, April 20, 2022, https://www.nytimes.com/2022/04 /20/nyregion/loneliness-epidemic.html.

Chapter 1: The Great Adventure

1. "The Top 5 Most Stressful Life Events and How to Handle Them," *The Science of Health* (blog), University Hospitals, July 2, 2015, https://www.uhhospitals.org/blog/articles/2015/07 /the-top-5-most-stressful-life-events.
2. Peter Farrelly and Bobby Farrelly, directors, *Dumb and Dumber*, 1994, Burbank, CA: New Line Cinema.

3. Jon Levy, *You're Invited: The Art and Science of Connection, Trust, and Belonging* (New York: Harper Business, 2021).

Chapter 2: WTF? (What the Family?)

1. "About Planet Fitness," Planet Fitness, accessed July 30, 2023, https://www.planetfitness.com/about-planet-fitness.
2. Jeremiah S. Chechik, director, *National Lampoon's Christmas Vacation*, 1989, Burbank, CA: Warner Bros. Pictures.
3. Michael Jackson, vocalist, "Man in the Mirror," by Glen Ballard and Siedah Garrett, on *Bad*, Epic Records, 1987.
4. Vanessa Thorpe, "Balcony Singing in Solidarity Spreads Across Italy During Lockdown," *Guardian*, March 14, 2020, https://www.theguardian.com/world/2020/mar/14/solidarity-balcony-singing-spreads-across-italy-during-lockdown.

Chapter 3: Table of Honor

1. Gary Portnoy, vocalist, "*Cheers* Theme (Where Everybody Knows Your Name)" by Gary Portnoy and Judy Hart-Angelo, 1983.
2. The Lucky Few Foundation, accessed August 1, 2023, https://theluckyfewfoundation.org/.
3. Sebastian Junger, *Tribe: On Homecoming and Belonging* (New York: Hachette, 2016), 127.
4. Sanjana Gupta, "What's the Difference Between Hearing and Listening?" VeryWell Mind, updated February 23, 2023, https://www.verywellmind.com/hearing-vs-listening-what-s-the-difference-5196734.
5. Emily Vogels, Risa Gelles-Watnick, and Navid Massarat, "Teens, Social Media and Technology 2022," Pew Research Center, August 10, 2022, https://www.pewresearch.org/internet/2022/08/10/teens-social-media-and-technology-2022/.
6. Emilie Le Beau Lucchesi, "What Is Smartphone Addiction and Is It Fueling Mental Health Problems?" *Discover*, March 7, 2023, https://www.discovermagazine.com/mind/what-is-smartphone-addiction-and-is-it-fueling-mental-health-problems.

Chapter 4: Excuse the Mess

1. Steven Spielberg, director, *Hook*, 1991, Culver City, CA: TriStar Pictures.

Chapter 5: The Humility Factor

1. Online Etymology Dictionary, s.v. "humble (*adj.*)," accessed August 2, 2023, https://www.etymonline.com/word/humble.

2. *Merriam-Webster Dictionary*, s.v. "humus (*n.*)," accessed August 2, 2023, https://www.merriam-webster.com/dictionary /humus.

3. Andrew Murray, *Humility: The Beauty of Holiness*, 2nd ed. (London: James Nisbet & Co., 1896), 12.

4. "As Partisan Hostility Grows, Signs of Frustration with the Two-Party System," Pew Research Center, August 9, 2022, https://www.pewresearch.org/politics/2022/08/09/as-partisan -hostility-grows-signs-of-frustration-with-the-two-party-system/.

5. Thomas Merton, *No Man Is an Island* (1955; repr. Boston: Shambhala, 2005), 119.

Chapter 6: Out of Bounds

1. TherapistAid, "What Are Personal Boundaries?" UHS-Berkeley, 2016, https://uhs.berkeley.edu/sites/default/files/relationships _personal_boundaries.pdf.

2. See, for example, Matthew 14:23; Mark 1:35; John 6:15; Luke 5:16.

Chapter 7: The Big B

1. Drew Weisholtz, "Brené Brown Opens Up About How Long Grief Lasts: 'It Takes As Long As It Takes,'" Today.com, March 31, 2022, https://www.today.com/health/mind-body/brene-brown -talks-long-grief-lasts-rcna22395.

Chapter 8: Drop Off the Baggage

1. Quoted in Alex Pattakos and Elain Dundon, *Prisoners of Our Thoughts*, 3rd ed. (Oakland, CA: Berrett-Koehler Publishers, Inc., 2017), 24, 147.

2. Lisa Firestone, "Forgiveness: The Secret to a Healthy Relationship," PsychAlive, accessed August 3, 2023, https://www.psychalive.org/forgiveness-the-secret-to-a-healthy-relationship/.

3. Firestone, "Forgiveness."

4. Henri Nouwen with Michael J. Christensen and Rebecca Laird, *Spiritual Direction: Wisdom for the Long Walk of Faith* (New York: HarperCollins, 2006), 120.

Chapter 9: Service with a Smile

1. Marc Forster, *A Man Called Otto*, 2022, Culver City, CA: Columbia Pictures.

2. Marianna Pogosyan, "In Helping Others, You Help Yourself," Psychology Today, May 30, 2018, https://www.psychologytoday.com/us/blog/between-cultures/201805/in-helping-others-you-help-yourself.

3. Jawahar Lalla, "The Tale of Two Seas," Times of India, February 7, 2021, https://timesofindia.indiatimes.com/readersblog/jblblogs/the-tale-of-two-seas-29568/.

Epilogue: Back to Risk

1. Nightbirde, vocalist, "It's Okay," written by Nightbirde (Jane Kristen Marczewski), 2021, https://www.nightbirde.co/lyrics/itsok.

2. Bronnie Ware, *The Top Five Regrets of the Dying: A Life Transformed by the Dearly Departing* (London: Hay House, 2012), 37.

3. Susie Steiner, "Top Five Regrets of the Dying," *The Guardian*, February 1, 2012, https://www.theguardian.com/lifeandstyle/2012/feb/01/top-five-regrets-of-the-dying.

About the
Authors

Julie and Chris Bennett are the founders of Welcome Home Lifestyle, which exists to create and promote content that celebrates all things family.

Their love for people and entertainment led them to relocate from Oklahoma to Los Angeles in 2018. Both Julie and Chris are graduates of Baylor University and have spent the majority of their twenty-three years of marriage working in vocational ministry. Through overwhelming challenges they have learned how to fight for the things that matter and devote themselves to helping others do the same.

Alongside their passion for building belonging for others, they love nothing more than spending time at home with their four kids.

The Bennetts live in Malibu, California, where Chris serves as lead pastor of Vintage Church.